Chocolate Unwrapped

TASTE & ENJOY THE WORLD'S FINEST CHOCOLATE

Sarah Jane Evans

PAVILION

Author's dedication: For Richard, Consola and Seraphina, with all my love

First published in 2010 by Pavilion Books

An imprint of Anova Books Company Ltd
10 Southcombe Street, London W14 0RA

www.anovabooks.com

Commissioning Editor Fiona Holman
Editor Maggie Ramsay
Designers Georgina Hewitt and John Heritage

A CIP catalogue for this book is available from the British Library.

ISBN 978-1-86205-859-0

Reproduction by Rival Colour Ltd, UK
Printed and bound by Toppan Leefung Co. Ltd, China

Reader's note:

* Cacao ('ka-kow') is the word used in this book for the tree, its pods and the unfermented beans.
  Cocoa is the word to describe the beans after fermenting and roasting, and all the subsequent
  by-products such as nibs, powder and butter.

* Countries are referred to in the text and on the maps by their contemporary names, following
  UN usage. Names on the chocolate bars may follow local usage.

* Part 2 Chocolate directory pages 62–227: producers are listed in alphabetical order using their
  full name. e.g. Enric Rovira is listed under 'E' and L'Artigiano di Gardini under 'L'. Packaging on
  the bars themselves may emphasise only one part of the name or an abbreviated version.

Captions
Page 1: A basket of Ecuadorian Nacional cacao pods (Kallari).
Page 2: Cacao tree (1993) by British artist, Liz Wright.
Pages 8–9: Sacks of dried cacao beans ready for shipping out of Madagascar (François Pralus).

Contents

Introduction

This is the first book to talk in any detail about chocolate and its flavours. It was inspired by the recent explosion in the number of bars, also called tablets, and their producers. Specialist chocolate shops are opening up around the world, their shelves filled with seriously chic wrapped bars. Thanks to web retailers, chocolate lovers in the most distant places can stay in touch.

How then do you begin to decide what to buy? This is where *Chocolate Unwrapped* comes in. Start by turning to the tasting section (see pages 57–61) to understand the process. Then dip into the directory that forms the core of this book (see pages 62–227). I have chosen a 70% bar (or similar) from each producer to highlight the style of each company. Find a bar that you know and like. Read my aroma and tasting notes on the bar. Then take a look at the tasting symbols in the profile of that bar: in the left-hand column are the light, floral, fruity, honeyed characters; in the right-hand column are the weightier, spicier, toasty, tannic qualities. (See also the sample profile on page 60.) Now find another bar with similar characteristics and start exploring. Alternatively, read first about a bar you have wanted to try, and learn more about the story of the producer. The shops and websites listed on page 234 will help you find a place to buy. I should add that the world of chocolate bars is constantly changing. New producers are starting up and existing ones extending their ranges and redesigning their packaging to keep up with competition. If you find a flavour or a producer that you particularly like please let me know at *www.sarahjaneevans.co.uk*.

I am an unreconstructed chocolate fan. I grew up enjoying traditional British milk chocolate bars. However, I was aware that there was a different world of chocolate because my father had a cache of Lindt and Bonnat bars in his desk. Much later, I spent more than a decade as associate editor of *BBC Good Food* magazine, thinking about flavours, how to distinguish between them, and how to describe them clearly. I then became a Master of Wine. Among other things, this qualification requires you to consider aromas, flavours and textures carefully and assess wines objectively, ignoring personal prejudice. These skills transfer themselves perfectly to fine chocolate, which has so many similarities with fine wine.

I am using the word 'fine' deliberately. You may find that some of your favourite bars are missing from this A–Z directory. This may be because they did not fit the initial definition of fine chocolate: the bars should have no vegetable fat other than cocoa butter; they should have a minimum cocoa content of 30% for milk chocolate and 60% for dark; they should be made from cacao beans whose quality and provenance have been considered; and they should contain no artificial flavourings, such as vanillin – genuine vanilla is, of course, permitted. I have taken these requirements from the Academy of Chocolate (*www.academyofchocolate.org.uk*), of which I am one of the founder members. Our aim is to promote the greater understanding of fine chocolate. We encourage everyone to discover fine chocolate in all its delicious diversity, and also to think more deeply about where their chocolate comes from, how it is made, and by whom.

Chocolate is nothing if not diverse. Among the producers in *Chocolate Unwrapped* are some who own their own estates and make their own chocolate, sometimes in the place of origin. There are an increasing number of 'bean-to-bar' producers, who make chocolate from beans that they have imported. Then there are a few who import cocoa mass or liquor (the ground nibs) and mix, stir and refine it (the process known as conching) until the flavours have developed and the textures changed. The majority of producers, however, buy finished chocolate – which professionals call couverture – and re-melt it, temper it, and perhaps blend and flavour it to create their own bars. The problem for chocolate lovers is that producers are not always transparent. In the search for transparency I have talked to many producers and chocolate experts, and there can be conflicting opinions. I am immensely grateful to everyone who shared their expertise (see Acknowledgements page 240) and any errors are entirely mine.

From bean to bar, *Chocolate Unwrapped* introduces this sumptuous world of fine chocolate, from its earliest history to its contemporary deliciousness, and the creative people behind the bars. I encourage you to explore the many flavours of chocolate and to unwrap the actual and metaphorical layers beneath the packaging.

Sarah Jane Evans

ONE

THE STORY OF
CHOCOLATE

HISTORY OF CHOCOLATE

Take a bite of a chocolate bar. Besides the pleasure it gives, chocolate leads us time and again on a journey. It makes remarkable links with geography, history, society, politics, economics. A bite of chocolate links us through time and space with cacao's origins in the shrinking tropical rainforests of the Amazon basin. The bar's other main ingredient, sugar, reaches back in the same way to colonial politics, and to the slave labour that has dominated sugar and cacao production for centuries.

Above: This Mayan cacao deity with blue beads wears the pod with pride.

There is also an element of mystery. How could chocolate have been invented? The original transformation of cacao and the release of the myriad flavours that go to make chocolate will forever remain conjecture, just like the transformation of the coffee berry to a cup of espresso. Allen M Young, in his book *The Chocolate Tree, A Natural History of Cacao*, speculates that:

Somewhere in Central America, a thousand or more years ago, a Mayan Indian picks the odd, football-shaped fruit jutting from the trunk and branches of a smooth-barked tree of the rain forest. Perhaps the fruit, encased in a hard, fibrous pod, is a bit past its prime – the normally refreshing white pulp slightly fermented, and the almond-like seeds, or beans, dried out. Perhaps the Indian spits the seeds, or tosses the entire fruit into a cook fire. As the beans roast, he is riveted by the aroma we now associate with hot fudge, simmering cocoa, freshly baked brownies, or a newly opened box of Switzerland's finest.

FROM OLMEC TO MAYA

When did chocolate start to make itself indispensable to humanity? The story starts in the far distant past and develops amid much theory and anecdote. In their important and absorbing book, *The True History of Chocolate*, anthropologists Sophie and Michael Coe estimate that the consumption of wild cacao may date back to well before the Mayans, perhaps as far as 1500BC. They trace it to the Olmec people of Meso-America, living in the Mexican highlands and the valley of Mexico. Linguistic analysis suggests that the word for cacao, *kakawa*, is derived from the Mixe-Zoquean language, and this links it to the Olmecs who first domesticated cacao.

As the Olmec civilisation declined, the Maya rose to prominence. The Mayans established an extensive, impressive culture that spread across what are now Belize, Honduras, Guatemala and southern Mexico, building stone pyramids and houses. They inhabited prime cacao land, populated by what is still regarded as the finest cacao, Criollo. They took cacao seriously and their artworks depict their leaders and priests with cacao trees and pods. Mayan pottery and frescoes show the ritual preparation of the drink, from grinding, crushing and pulverising the beans; steeping and soaking the powder; filtering the liquid; and then splashing it from a height from one beaker to another, which created a foam of bubbles on the top of the drink. The Mayans buried their dead with useful items for the afterlife, and these included containers for chocolate. Traces of theobromine and caffeine, two of the active ingredients of chocolate, have been found in the containers.

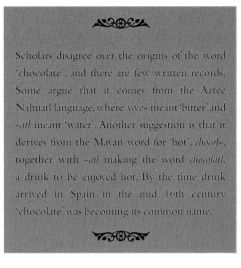

Scholars disagree over the origins of the word 'chocolate', and there are few written records. Some argue that it comes from the Aztec Nahuatl language, where *xoco-* meant 'bitter' and *-atl* meant 'water'. Another suggestion is that it derives from the Mayan word for 'hot', *chocol-*, together with *-atl* making the word *chocolatl*, a drink to be enjoyed hot. By the time drink arrived in Spain in the mid 16th century 'chocolate' was becoming its common name.

It is clear that in early times cacao was a luxury, associated with divine worship. Surviving documents show illustrations of gods with cacao beans. Chocolate's religious appeal is easily understood. The cacao tree growing under the forest canopy with its myriad white flowers and its pods sprouting directly from its trunk is a miraculous sight. The drink made from it was nourishing and stimulated the brain. Not only was cacao nourishing, it was thought to have healing qualities, and even perhaps aphrodisiac powers, an idea that still has echoes in advertising today.

The Mayan civilization remained powerful for more than 600 years, but by the ninth century AD it was collapsing after a series of internal wars. By the time Christopher Columbus arrived on his final trip to the Americas in 1502, the culture was more or less defunct.

COLUMBUS FAILS TO DISCOVER CHOCOLATE

Columbus landed off Honduras, on the island of Guanaja. Legend has it that he was met by the local people in a huge dugout canoe full of goods, including one of their most valuable items, cacao beans. It was one of those fleeting moments in history that has, with hindsight, taken on far greater significance. This was the discovery of a food whose appeal led to the movement of populations, as plantation workers were enslaved over centuries, and the creation of global brands. However, the first Europeans missed the moment in their search for gold. Columbus's son Ferdinand recollected later the appearance of these almond-shaped beans:

> They seemed to hold these almonds at a great price; for when they were brought on board ship together with their goods, I observed that when any of these almonds fell, they all stopped to pick it up, as though an eye had fallen.

Cacao was, as scholars have noted, the gold that grew on trees. It – or clay representations of the beans – was a coinage. Columbus was not impressed.

However, he did learn of the Aztecs and their leader Montezuma, who came to power that same year. Montezuma's realm extended from the Gulf of Mexico down to Nicaragua, and its heart was its great capital Tenochtitlán, based where Mexico City is today. Montezuma II (correctly named as Motecuhzoma Xocoyotzin) was a powerful despot. As befitted a king, he drank *cacahuatl* (the Aztec word for the drink made from cacao). Given the value of cacao as coinage, Montezuma was literally drinking gold.

The fine Criollo cacao he enjoyed did not grow locally. The beans had to be imported to the city from the outer parts of his empire, from the Pacific coast of Chiapas and Guatemala; this added to the perception of cacao's value. Chocolate was a drink that nourished Aztec warriors as well as their kings. Foreshadowing the Quakers in the 19th century, the Aztec authorities favoured *cacahuatl*

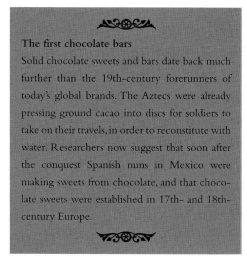

The first chocolate bars
Solid chocolate sweets and bars date back much further than the 19th-century forerunners of today's global brands. The Aztecs were already pressing ground cacao into discs for soldiers to take on their travels, in order to reconstitute with water. Researchers now suggest that soon after the conquest Spanish nuns in Mexico were making sweets from chocolate, and that chocolate sweets were established in 17th- and 18th-century Europe.

because it was not alcoholic. *Octli*, from the agave plant, was mildly intoxicating, and the penalty for drunkenness was death. The Aztecs liked to drink their chocolate cold, and they sometimes sweetened it with honey, presaging the way the rest of the world was to enjoy chocolate. They might also have added a dye, to colour the drinker's mouth red – and this dye (annatto, or achiote) is still used in Central America today. Historians suggest that the Aztecs saw the liquid chocolate as a parallel to blood, just as they drew a parallel between the shape of the cocoa pod and the shape of the human heart.

The enterprising Spanish captain Hernán Cortés, who led an expedition from Cuba to the Mexican mainland in 1519, believed that the Americas were the place to make his fortune. He showed more curiosity than Columbus in cacao, and the priests who travelled with him were equally interested. They were the ones who found out about the claimed stimulant and health properties of the dark 'almonds', and who would subsequently bring the recipes back to Europe.

The Spanish fortune-hunter could not fail to be impressed by Montezuma's magnificent empire, and it spurred his determination to conquer the Aztec people. In just two years the Spaniards sacked the great city of Tenochtitlán. Montezuma was finally brought down by the mix of guile, deceit and violence that typically marked the progress of the conquistadores. Whether he died at the hands of his own people or the Spaniards is uncertain. One story, surely purveyed by the Spanish Church, is that he lingered for ten days, converted to Christianity and asked for his daughters to be brought up in the faith.

Above: Montezuma, seated on his woven reed throne and wearing the royal cloak, sends his ambassadors to the conquistadores, as recorded by the Spanish priest Diego Durán (1579).

The survivor of that conflict, Hernán Cortés, has not been treated well by history, and he found himself obliged to travel regularly to and from Spain to defend himself and his reputation to the Emperor Charles V – and apologise for his failure to find the expected gold. He died in 1547 in his palace on the outskirts of Seville, a rich man but not universally popular. Thus passed the first two significant figures in the history of chocolate.

CHOCOLATE CONQUERS EUROPE

Hernán Cortés brought plenty out of the Americas to fascinate the Spanish court, but cacao was not top of his treasures. The first record of chocolate's formal introduction to royalty was in 1544, when it was brought by a group of Kekchi Maya on a visit to the future Philip II of Spain; among other items, they brought with them cacao, maize, sarsaparilla and chillies. In a relatively short time, and despite the scarcity of the raw material, Spain transformed *cacahuatl* into a delicacy capable of conquering Europe. It did this with new recipes, adding sugar to make it more palatable; with new equipment, the *molinillo*; and by creating a new ritual, the taking of chocolate.

The Spanish chocolate drink contained a variety of flavourings, in addition to sugar. There were the sweet spices – cinnamon and vanilla – and chillies, as well as almonds or hazelnuts, and there might be aniseed, powdered roses, orange water and annatto (which besides colouring the drink red gave it a light floral scent).

In the Americas cacao had been ground on a stone *metate* – as it still is today in many places – before being mixed with water, and then poured from a height to assist the blending of the water and the powder; this created a froth which could be poured off to reveal the drink, or simply sipped through, like a modern-day cappuccino. A Spanish traveller to the New World in the early 16th century, Gonzalo Fernández de Oviedo, had observed that heated cooked chocolate produced 'an excellent oil', which rose to the top and could be skimmed away and used. The Spaniards in

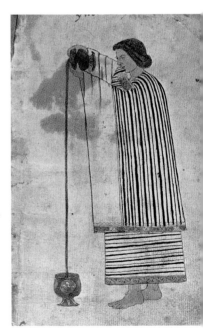

Above: A Mexican noblewoman prepares the foaming chocolate in a painted cup (1553).

Mexico made their own contribution to the blending process with the *molinillo*, a swizzle stick with a grooved head. This stick eventually became part of the European chocolate ritual.

Spain held on to its chocolate for more than half a century before it crossed the Pyrenees and the Mediterranean to spread into other parts of Europe; for a long time it was more or less exclusive to the nobility and religious houses. Visitors to the Spanish court encountered chocolate at the public displays of the Inquisition; both the inquisitors and the victims of torture and execution were served the drink.

Manière dont les habitans de la nouvelle Espagne preparent le Chcao pour le Chocolat.

Above: 'How the natives of new Spain prepared cacao for chocolate', a French engraving of 1591 showing how quickly the new drink became part of European culture.

The Catholic Church faced a dilemma. On the one hand their missionaries in the Americas had identified chocolate's nutritional benefits and passed on their knowledge to the Old World. On the other hand, chocolate was both nourishing and tempting, and disrupted the Lenten fast of 40 days and nights. Finally, Cardinal Brancaccio of the Vatican came to the decision in 1662 that liquid chocolate did not break the fast.

Francesco Redi, the physician to the court of Cosimo III de' Medici, Grand Duke of Tuscany, experimented with ambitious combinations of flavourings, including the heady perfumes of musk and ambergris. It is no wonder that a cup of chocolate was a popular vehicle for poisoning. Legend has it that in 1774 Pope Clement XIV was poisoned with chocolate, by the Jesuits whom he had opposed. By this date Italy's chefs had become thoroughly enchanted with chocolate. A cookery book of the period offered such creative cuisine as liver dipped in chocolate and flour and fried; black polenta made with chocolate breadcrumbs, butter, almonds and cinnamon; and chocolate pudding with veal marrow and candied fruit.

As for France, there is one tradition that chocolate came as part of a royal dowry. The young Spanish princess Anne of Austria was sent in 1615 in a dynastic marriage to the equally young Louis XIII of France. It was not a happy marriage, and it is suggested that chocolate was one of the Queen's

Above: The chocolate ritual as enjoyed in Spain a century or so after its arrival in Europe – the wooden swizzle stick or *molinillo* with its ridged head (far left), long-handled pot and two-handled cup – painted in 1640 by Juan de Zurbarán, son of the more famous Francisco de Zurbarán.

consolations. Another story attributes the fashion for chocolate to the enthusiasm of Cardinal Alphonse de Richelieu (older brother of the more famous Cardinal Richelieu, the king's chief minister), who was advised by his doctor to drink the nourishing liquid to improve his health.

Initially the royal ladies drank chocolate in private, as it was thought to be unladylike to consume it in public. However, during the marriage of the Spanish Maria Teresa to Louis XIV, the chocolate habit was established at court, and became the drink that smoothed the path of business. Despite this, Louis XIV was not a fan.

By 1659, chocolate was sufficiently popular that the first French chocolatier, David Chaillou, set up shop in Paris, having won a royal monopoly for the 'sole privilege for 23 years of making, retailing and selling in all towns of the Kingdom a certain composition known as chocolate, in liquid form or as pastilles or in any other form that he may please.'

REFINING THE RITUAL

The Marqués de Mancera, Spain's Viceroy of Peru between 1639 and 1648, invented the chocolate cup and saucer. At first, the Spanish court had drunk its chocolate like the Aztecs, from hollowed-out gourds or clay bowls called *jícaras*. The story is that the thoughtful Marqués was horrified to see a lady at one of his receptions accidentally spill a *jícara* of chocolate on her dress and, in the words of Sophie and Michael Coe,

> determined to find a better way to take the drink. He had a Lima silversmith make a plate or saucer with a collar-like ring in the middle, into which a small cup would sit without being able to slip. Thus was born the *mancerina*, eventually to be manufactured in porcelain by European potters.

The *mancerina* soon caught on. Mme d'Aulnoy, a Frenchwoman visiting the Spanish court in 1679, wrote:

> they presented next the Chocolate, each cup of porcelain on a saucer of agate garnished with gold, with the sugar in the bowl of the same. There was iced chocolate, another hot, and another with Milk and Eggs; one took it with a Biscuit, or rather with dry small Buns…beside this, they take it with so much pepper and so many spices, that it is impossible they don't burn themselves up.

Above: In the 1730s the elegant drink even became a pattern on French silk.

According to one collector, it was the English who added the lid to the cup to keep the chocolate warm, and the French who introduced the tray to hold a set of cups. The French are also credited with adding the handle on the side of the silver chocolate pot or chocolatière, to enable a steady hold when spinning the whisk inside the lid. This whisk – the descendant of the original *molinillo* – was important for beating the thick, rich liquid before pouring. The saucer for the cup eventually became enlarged to hold a biscuit or cake. The cup itself often had two handles. The *trembleuse*, as it became known, was just the thing for an old lady with a shaky or trembling hand, or even on board ship.

With this display of finery, chocolate was a drink for high society. Mme de Sévigné, the celebrated letter-writer of 17th-century France, was loyal to her chocolatière, and in 1671 wrote to her daughter, Mme de Grignan, the typical letter of a parent unable to let go of a grown-up child: 'If you are not feeling well, if you have not slept, chocolate will revive you. But you have no chocolatière! I think of that again and again. How will you manage?' She continued to worry about her daughter, but changed her mind about chocolate later that same year. When Mme de Grignan was pregnant, her mother wrote: 'My dear, my beautiful child, I do beg you not to drink chocolate. In your present condition it would prove fatal to you.' But it seemed that Mme de Grignan had not got the message. In October, mother wrote once more, determined to terrify her daughter into giving up the habit: 'The Marquise de Coëtlogon drank so much chocolate when she was expecting last year that she was brought to bed of a little boy as black as the devil, who died.'

HOT CHOCOLATE HOUSES

Chocolate became increasingly popular during the 17th and 18th centuries: men enjoyed the drink at the chocolate and coffee houses that flourished in towns and cities throughout Europe, from Vienna to Amsterdam, and both sexes took chocolate at home. Nonetheless, it remained a drink for the wealthy; servants laboured over its preparation, but seldom tasted it.

In England, chocolate was definitely a social drink. Tea and coffee had already arrived; all three are stimulating substances. No wonder late 17th-century London was awash with chocolate houses and coffee houses where men could meet and discuss politics. The famous diarist Pepys gave an enthusiastic report:

> 'About noon out with Commissioner Pett, and he and I into a Coffee-house to drink Jocolatte, very good!'
>
> SAMUEL PEPYS, LONDON, 24 NOVEMBER 1664

Some of London's coffee and chocolate houses continued into the 20th century; the most famous of these is White's (see illustration facing page), which opened in 1693 and remains to this day a gentlemen's club, though politically more conservative than when it opened its doors. The Cocoa Tree survived almost as long, but eventually closed in the early 20th century.

Sophie and Michael Coe make the point that while in France chocolate was, as so many things, a state monopoly, available only to the elite, in democratic England chocolate (and coffee, and tea) were available to anyone who could pay. Indeed it could be argued that the easy supply of chocolate and coffee, alongside free debate and discussion, was one reason why England avoided Revolution in the years of European agitation.

By the beginning of the 18th century, chocolate was beginning to appear as an ingredient in England's burgeoning literature of cookery. Recipes included chocolate creams and chocolate puffs.

Yet even a century later chocolate was still not universally appreciated in England. In London, William Tayler, a 30-year-old servant in the house of a rich widow in Mayfair, London, kept a diary in 1837 to record life in the house, and to improve his handwriting. He commented that for breakfast his employer and her daughter consumed 'hot rolls, dry toast, a loaf of fancy bread…'. In addition to tea, they also drank 'chocolate which is something like coffee but of a greasey and much richer nature'. What Tayler did not know is that inventors had been working on machines to remove some of the 'greasey' cocoa butter, and that in the Netherlands Coenraad Van Houten had already patented such a press, and had developed a process that was going to make chocolate altogether more palatable.

A DUTCH INVENTION

The advance of chocolate began to accelerate around 1750 as it kept pace with the industrial revolution. The United States' first chocolate factory opened in 1765, run by Dr James Baker and John Hannan. The arrival of the steam engine enabled consistent, bulk production. In Europe a flurry of chocolatiers sprang up – in England, France, Spain, Germany, Switzerland, the Netherlands – and factories opened to feed the demand. In Germany, the Swiss Josty

Above: Thomas Rowlandson's 'The White House' (1787), with chocolate pot ignored.

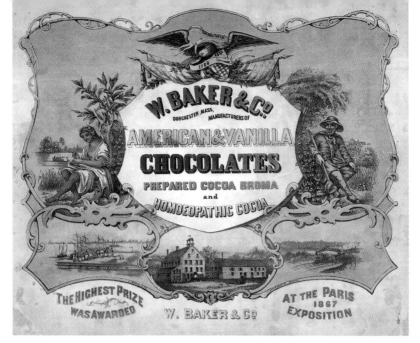

Above: Cocoa has never lost its 'bound to do you good' reputation.

brothers opened their factory in Berlin in 1792; in France, Menier was founded in 1816, Poulain in 1848; in Switzerland, Cailler was founded in 1819, and Suchard started up in 1826.

The aroma and flavour of drinking chocolate were irresistible, but one thing spoiled its elegance: fat, or rather, cocoa butter which accounts for around 50 per cent of the bean. When the ground particles were mixed with hot water, the fat rose unappealingly to the surface. Producers had tried to remove the fat in various ways, but Coenraad Van Houten, working in his chocolate factory in Amsterdam in the early 19th century, developed a hydraulic press that removed about half of the cocoa butter from the nibs. The resulting pressed cake could then be milled to make a powder. His next step was to find a way for the cocoa powder to disperse better in the hot liquid. In 1828 he patented a process for treating the cacao beans with an alkaline liquid during roasting – a process that became known as 'Dutching'. This also made the chocolate darker. Ever since, thanks to clever marketing, the Dutch have appeared as the purveyors of fireside warmth and comfort.

One of the great names of English chocolate, Fry's of Bristol, was founded in the middle of the 18th century by the Quaker Joseph Fry. His son, also called Joseph, introduced a steam engine to the family business in 1795. It was the third-generation Francis Fry's contribution to the world of chocolate that was to go down in history. In 1847, building on Van Houten's defatting process, Fry found the way to blend cocoa liquor (the paste of ground roasted cacao beans) and sugar with cocoa butter to produce a liquid that could be poured into moulds to set and create bars of eating chocolate. Fry's discovery was being mirrored in France and Italy. This was dark chocolate, and it must have been a reasonably challenging substance in terms of its grainy texture and bitterness. A sweeter treat was *gianduja* (pronounced 'jan-dooya'), a confection of ground hazelnuts and chocolate invented in 1861 by Isidore Caffarel in Turin, Italy.

Solid chocolate for eating was a success around the world. In the United States, Baker's German's Sweet Chocolate appeared in 1852, named after its creator Sam German, a Baker's employee. On the West Coast, the California gold rush made San Francisco a boom town. Italian-born Domingo Ghirardelli, who had established himself as a chocolate and coffee merchant in Peru, was quick to exploit the boom and set up shop in San Francisco in 1852. French chocolatier Etienne Guittard (see page 136) followed in 1868.

Despite its increasing appeal, chocolate, like so many foods then, was widely adulterated. Instead of cocoa butter a selection of cheaper fats was used, and starches were added to bulk out the more expensive ingredients. A survey in the UK medical journal, *The Lancet*, in 1850, which analysed a range of foods, found that just over half of their sample of chocolate contained red ochre from ground bricks. Food Laws of 1860 and 1872 began to put an end to such practices.

SMOOTHING THE WAY

The invention of the milk chocolate bar came about indirectly. In 1727 an Englishman, Nicholas Sanders, made and sold a nutritious chocolate drink with milk following the recipe of the distinguished surgeon Sir Hans Sloane. In Switzerland, some 150 years later, Henri Nestlé, who was working with baby foods, invented powdered milk, by evaporating the water. His neighbour Daniel Peter was then able to blend this dried product with cocoa liquor, sugar and cocoa butter to make a solid, milk-flavoured bar.

Above: The old ads are the best: dogs and chocolate never fail. This one dates back to 1911 and shows the Swiss Alps' long association with chocolate.

Five years later, in 1880, Rodolphe Lindt, also in Switzerland, transformed our experience of chocolate, producing a chocolate bar with a superb silkiness. The machine he invented was the conch, or conche, named after the shell of the same name. It is mesmerising to watch.

Inside a large deep trough there is an equally large roller, moving restlessly through a sea of warm liquid chocolate. The roller gradually breaks down the cocoa particles and coats them evenly with cocoa butter. For our tongues to perceive a velvet smoothness the particles need to be smaller than 30 microns (1000 microns = 1mm). In addition, in the process of aerating the chocolate, some water and acids are evaporated, reinforcing the softness on the palate. The invention was apparently one of life's chance discoveries. The story goes that a machine was left on overnight by mistake. This sounds plausible. What is particularly interesting is that some of the most passionate producers today own conches that are technically antique. Not for them the shining, easy-to-clean stainless steel; a time-worn conch is the artisan's choice.

Switzerland in the middle of the 19th century was a centre of chocolate invention. Snowy Swiss mountains became associated with chocolate, and it's an association that persists, despite the fact that a tropical origin is so much more important than a Swiss machine.

During most of the 19th century, chocolate was sold mainly by specialist confectioners and confiseries in the towns. Rural consumers, familiar with coloured jellies and boiled sugar sweets, took a bit of getting used to chocolate. In her semi-autobiographical account of her early life, *Lark Rise to Candleford*, Flora Thompson recalled an English village feast in the 1880s:

> One year, side by side with the gingerbread babies, stood a box filled with thin, dark-brown slabs packed in pink paper. 'What is that brown sweet?' asked Laura, spelling out the word 'Chocolate'. A visiting cousin…already knew its name. 'Oh, that's chocolate,' he said off-handedly. 'But don't buy any; it's for drinking. They have it for breakfast in France.' A year or two later, chocolate was a favourite sweet even in a place as remote as the hamlet.

By the end of the 19th century, chocolate bars had become affordable and available. Chocolate could be produced industrially and transported easily through national networks of railways. The chocolate bar was poised to become a favourite in times of war and peace. To encourage demand the manufacturers made good use of advertising and marketing, with appealing images, hopeful slogans and brightly coloured wrappers. Gold printing and metal foils helped the new confection to stand out. This lyrical and romantic approach marked the beginning of a golden age of chocolate advertising. The 20th century was to prove memorable for its bold sloganising of chocolate – from 'A Mars a day helps you work, rest and play' to 'The Milky Bars are on me', as well as for its positioning as a private indulgence. Yet advertising and promotion were also to become intrusive as brands fought for our attention through every form of marketing technique.

MILK CHOCOLATE EMPIRES

At the very turn of the century, on 10 August 1900, Milton Hershey sold the caramel business he had built up over the previous 20 years for $1 million; he used the money to buy land near Harrisburg, Pennsylvania, where he could build a chocolate factory and a model community for his workers and their families. Hershey also built a remarkably successful school for orphans and the underprivileged. He later transferred ownership of the chocolate company to the school Trust: effectively the governors had the final say over the business. This was a remarkable structure for a food company.

Milton then turned his mind to the latest trend – milk chocolate: milk was usefully abundant in the rich Pennsylvania farmland. In her book *The Chocolate Wars*, Joël Glenn Brenner tells the story of how he used to work 16-hour days, with many setbacks, attempting to perfect a milk chocolate that he could manufacture in bulk. He eventually worked out how to make a bar, but the method he chose resulted in a slightly sour flavour, and a distinctly grainy texture. This became the familiar local favourite but it could not compete internationally in any territories where companies with different flavour profiles such as Cadbury or Lindt were established. Children in chocolate-eating countries learn the flavours young, and remain loyal to those flavours as adults.

Hershey was never troubled by this, for sales grew in the United States in an apparently unstoppable fashion. During the Second World War Hershey captured the lucrative military market with a bar that did not melt: Sara Jayne-Stanes reports in *Chocolate: the definitive guide* that after Pearl Harbor 500,000 of these field rations were produced every 24 hours. Milton Hershey died in

Above: A 1900s collector's card: a century later we are still debating child labour in chocolate.

1945 and did not live to see the globalisation of chocolate brands. As a man who never saw the point of advertising or marketing, he would have been astonished at the investment required to launch and sustain a brand today.

It took the Mars family to teach chocolate producers about marketing. Forrest Mars learnt how to make chocolate the easy way – he went to be an ordinary worker on the shop floor in Switzerland and watched the experts. Ever after, he – like Willy Wonka – had a very clear idea of the risks of espionage and the need to keep out prying eyes from the factory.

Forrest's father, Frank, opened his candy factory in Minnesota in 1911. Forrest set up his business in Slough, England, in 1932; his Mars bar was an instant success. Interestingly, his first Mars bars were coated with Cadbury's chocolate; at that time producers did not guard their recipes so fiercely. It was a clever move since his Mars Bar was cheaper than Cadbury's Dairy Milk, because it contained less chocolate.

In Europe the century began with the opening of Jean Tobler's factory, where Toblerone would be made; also in Switzerland, Max Felchlin began to produce chocolate in 1908. In Belgium, Leonidas was founded in 1910 and Callebaut the following year; the Draps family opened Godiva (see page 126) in Brussels in 1926. In Venezuela, El Rey (see page 116) was launched in 1929.

The middle years of the 20th century saw periods of innovation in chocolate confectionery, interrupted by wartime rationing and supply shortages worldwide. After the Second World War, as Europe was emerging from austerity, a number of important chocolate names were setting out in France: Michel Cluizel (see page 168) in 1948; Valrhona (see page 216), created in 1950 out of the former Chocolaterie de Vivarais; Bernachon (see page 82) in 1955. Twenty years later Robert Linxe opened his own business, the influential La Maison du Chocolat in Paris (see page 152). In 1984 Jean-Paul Hévin

Above: US GIs made friends everywhere with their chocolate bars (Germany, 1945).

(see page 140) went to work in Tokyo for a year, one of a growing number of exchanges reflecting the ever closer links between fine chocolatiers in France and Japan. In those years France's chocolatiers were the leaders of the fine chocolate market, while the Belgian companies came to be seen as the popular luxury option. Hershey and Mars meanwhile dominated the global market for confectionery chocolate.

The century ended, as actively as it had begun, in a flurry of takeovers and mergers. Godiva was sold to Campbell's Soup, and then in 2008 to the Turkish company Yildiz Holding. Green & Black's (see page 128) was snaffled by Cadbury Schweppes; Dagoba (see page 106) and Scharffen Berger (see page 200) were gobbled up by Hershey's.

Yet while the global brands continued to hold the vast majority of the market, the 1980s and 90s saw the first stirrings of a movement of artisan chocolatiers, and of a fascination with the origin of the beans. From the mid-1980s Valrhona started to market bars from named regions. And in 1989 Lindt (see page 156) launched a 70% bar, making it the first major manufacturer to declare a cocoa solids percentage. In 1995 Olivier de Loisy, formerly the managing director of Valrhona, started the Chocolaterie de l'Opéra (see page 229), sourcing beans directly from plantations. Knowledge about fine chocolate was beginning to spread – though at the same time Britain was insisting that the European Union continued to permit it to include up to 5 per cent vegetable fat in its chocolate (it won the case, which is why it is so important to read the list of ingredients on the bar).

THE 21ST-CENTURY RENAISSANCE

All of a sudden, chocolate is hot. High cocoa solids, single origin, single estate, organic, raw, antioxidant; in every shape and size – bars, bonbons, ganaches and the hot drink. A generation brought up on an abundance of sugar and fat and advertising and globalisation and consistency is seeking out chocolate with identity, with vintage variation and individuality. The takeover of Cadbury by Kraft in 2009 only highlighted the fact that chocolate is a commodity, and that people who care about creativity may want to seek out new producers.

The pages that follow highlight the most obvious aspect of the renaissance – bars. These are the pure expressions of a chocolatier's art. (I use the French word chocolatier to identify chocolate producers, whatever their country of origin.) Today's chocolatiers are a very varied selection. There are chocolatiers whose production is – or verges on – industrial. Some of these are companies

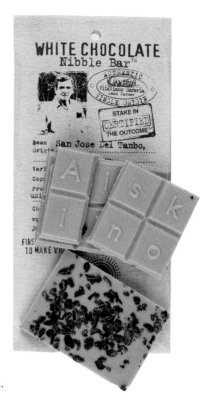

more than a century old, and others may not last out to the end of the year. There are former bankers, lawyers and computer geeks, who have turned a hobby into a career, or who were looking for a career and found chocolate. There are family businesses, and growers venturing to make their own bars rather than just sell on the beans.

None of these businesses can stand still. As consumers we insist on novelty, and producers cannot resist imitation. One person invents a Tonka bean bar, a chocolate with sea salt or a chilli chocolate, and suddenly everyone is copying them. Still, within the pages of this book there are creative producers who are managing to remain original.

One way of being different is to add texture. Nibs, the heart of the roasted, husked bean, have recently become popular for the way they make a lifted, bitter contrast to sweetened chocolate, in bars or as a decoration for truffles. Two of the more successful nib bars are Kaoka's organic 61% **Noir Éclats de Fèves de Cacao Caramelisés** (see page 145), which give a dart of bitter sweetness, and Michel Cluizel's **Grué** (see page 168). Some chocolatiers prefer the lazy look, sprinkling whole fruits, petals and nuts across the bar. The result looks charming, but does not always integrate satisfactorily. The latest ingredient to divide chocolate fans is 'space dust', known to children as popping candy; I am in the camp that would prefer to keep it on the confectionery shelf.

Chilli remains a popular addition to bars, though since it usually dominates the flavour of the chocolate and anything that comes after, I hope it falls from favour. Pepper, on the other hand, as used by Åkesson's (see page 64) can be successful. Other spices – cardamom, ginger, cinnamon – marry with chocolate far more harmoniously. Orange is an established partner, but the marrying of other fruits with chocolate has generally been less successful. Sea salted caramels and chocolate – so long as they are made with a mild, flaked salt and not an overpowering 'cooking' salt – are now a firm 21st-century favourite.

Filled chocolates are outside the remit of this book, but it must be noted that the century opened with a sensational blossoming in ganache-filled individual chocolates. While the large, indulgent, butter- and cream-filled chocolates of Belgium remain popular, creative chocolatiers have moved on to experiment with intense, complex, highly original flavours. Some of the wilder combinations parallel the work of imaginative chefs such as Ferrán Adriá, who took his restaurant, El Bulli, near Barcelona, to international fame. Indeed several of the current generation of chocolatiers trained as chefs before focusing their talents on chocolate. While some of the new flavours, such as cheese or anchovies, lack charm, others – using Japanese flavours such as yuzu (a citrus fruit), green tea, black vinegar – have a subtle elegance. Some producers have eschewed dairy altogether and make their ganaches – a blend of cream and chocolate – with water and chocolate instead. This can give a very intense chocolate 'hit'.

The effect of a water-based ganache depends on the quality of the chocolate, its cocoa solids and its origin or blend. Labelling chocolate with its percentage of cocoa solids has been a significant trend this century. It is widely believed that 'The higher the cocoa solids, the better the chocolate', yet this is not necessarily the case. A fine dark chocolate needs to have enough cocoa solids to give a pure chocolate flavour. Most producers make a bar with 70% cocoa solids, which is why I have chosen a 70% bar – or as near as possible – as the subject for the tasting notes in this book. My limit for enjoyment is usually 85%, though I have found a few producers who manage to create an enjoyable 85%, and even one at 100% (Domori, see page 114). As for milk chocolate, the recent move to 'dark milks' hovering between 45% and 64% is a great step forward. These are real chocolates, with a soothing milkiness.

An extension of high cocoa solids is raw chocolate, which has been processed at lower temperatures than normal. This falls into an alternative, 'health food' category, with passionate devotees, rather than the mainstream. For more about raw chocolate, see Pacari page 178.

Around the world artisan producers are popping up, and their approach to chocolate – and their stylish packaging – is being echoed by the big producers who need to keep up with the trends. There is no legal definition of artisan,

Right: Chocolate for today's armchair explorer: beautifully packaged, to enjoy with an atlas. These bars are from François Pralus.

but any skilled producer will be proud to offer one. It indicates careful selection of ingredients, hand production and small volumes. Underlying it all is a search for quality: quality of execution, exceptional melt, complex and lingering flavours, and individuality. Fine chocolate tastes of where it comes from, of its terroir, and of its manufacturer. Labelling bars with their country of origin has entered the mainstream – it is no longer unusual to see Peru, Ecuador or Venezuela on a wrapper. Single-estate chocolate now has the same glamour as wine from a top French château.

The latest fashion is bean-to-bar production. It represents a tiny percentage of the global market but has an influence far beyond its size. It can mean different things to different producers. Some own or have very close ties with a property, and manage every aspect of the production from cacao ('bean') to packaging ('bar'). This is in tune with the widespread desire for traceability. A very few producers also make their bars in the country of origin. The majority of bean-to-bar producers purchase beans to make into bars elsewhere.

It is worth remembering, however, that blending across regions or countries is a fine and subtle art. Take the Italian producer Amedei (see page 70): its single-estate **Chuao** is highly rated; yet its **Toscano** and **'9'** blends have just as many fans. A blend can even out the sharp edges, the seasonal variations, and is very often greater than the sum of its parts. Unfortunately the search for origin has given rise to a chocolate snobbism taking place over craftsmanship.

Terroir and chocolate

While Cortés was striding about South America in the early 16th century, Cistercian monks were planting vines in Burgundy and elsewhere. Over the centuries, observation has discovered the very best sites to such a degree that vineyards in parts of Burgundy can be defined to the last metre in terms of quality. The soil, the aspect to the sun, the height above sea level, the availability of water and the temperature difference between day and night – all these, together with the skill of the grower, make the difference between a good site and a great one. Whether the vineyard is in Burgundy or Bío Bío in Chile, the effect is the same; the only difference is that the Burgundians have had longer to practice and observe. In the world of cacao, the same holds true. The weather is central to terroir. It is important in wine, where frost, hail, or lack of sun can halve a vintage, and it can be devastating in chocolate. In tropical storms whole plantations can be damaged. The Grenada Chocolate Company (see page 130) took three years to recover from the devastation caused by Hurricane Ivan in 2004.

CHOCOLATE AND HEALTH

Is chocolate good for you? It's impossible to know whom to believe. The difficulty is that there is so little independent research. Siren voices from the chocolate industry tempt us with honeyed words, and studies of chocolate's possible health benefits always prove popular in the media. Consumer demand for foods that have a declared nutritional benefit has affected the chocolate business. Bars with 100% cocoa solids (and therefore more antioxidants) are increasingly seen, as are 'raw' chocolate bars.

Nevertheless the chocolate community has good reason to encourage more research, despite the fact that speaking out in favour of chocolate can seem like defending smoking in public. When it comes to dark chocolate, there is plenty of good news. In particular:

- Chocolate and cocoa powder contain high levels of flavonoids; these are the antioxidants also found in tea and red wine, and are helpful in protecting against cardiovascular disease. The processing of chocolate reduces the level of antioxidants. Informal research has shown that bars produced at the place of origin, using fairly primitive machinery, deliver a higher level of flavonoids than highly processed bars.

- Further research suggests that chocolate may be beneficial in relation to dementia, diabetes and breast cancer.

It is important to stress that the research does not relate to milk chocolate, or to an everyday selection of filled chocolates. The research is based on moderate consumption of dark chocolate – which is lower in sugar and fat than milk and filled chocolates. Just as with drinking wine, there is a positive benefit from limited regular consumption, but that benefit diminishes as consumption increases.

Right: 'Raw' does not have to mean 100% cocoa solids; this bar also contains evaporated cane juice (to sweeten), cacao butter and sunflower lecithin.

FROM BEAN TO BAR

Botanical gardens with glass houses in cold cities shelter the occasional lonely cacao trees as a monument to tropical explorers, botanical science and central heating. At the Royal Botanic Gardens at Kew in London, *Theobroma cacao* is classified quaintly as an economic plant, sounding like something out of Lewis Carroll's *Alice in Wonderland*. Its fellows in this group include coffee, cotton and rubber, as well as its regular companion in the plantations, the banana tree, which provides cacao with shade and shelter.

The cacao tree flourishes in the tropics between 20° North and 20° South of the Equator. Within this ribbon round the earth lie plenty of diverse origins, from Venezuela to Vietnam. *T. cacao* probably originated in the Amazon River basin, and gradually moved north, establishing itself across Central America. Some trees were shipped by man to new sites, others moved naturally with animal carriers. John Scharffenberger (see page 200) reckons that hippos were among the more discriminating of cacao's vectors.

Cacao's adventures beyond the Americas are all based on empire. The Spanish took it to the Philippines, as well as controlling plantations in Mexico, Colombia and parts of the Caribbean. The Dutch took cacao to Indonesia. Britain's

cacao empire stretched from Trinidad and Jamaica in the Caribbean to Sri Lanka, France's to Madagascar. The Germans took cacao to New Guinea and Cameroon. Portuguese settlers on the islands of São Tomé and Príncipe, off West Africa, had grown sugar there since the 16th century; coffee and cacao were introduced in the early 19th century. From here, cacao was taken to the Gold Coast (now Ghana) and the Côte d'Ivoire.

Today 70 per cent of the world's cacao is grown in West Africa and feeds our appetites for most chocolate confectionery. In contrast, Venezuela's production is tiny – less than 1 per cent of the world's cacao output – but the top quality of its cacao has resulted in political dramas over the ownership of its plantations.

Above: The magic of cacao: the flowers and the pods grow directly from the trunk of the tree. This is in Bolivia.

THE CACAO FAMILY

To start at the top of the botanical tree, the family name is *Sterculiaceae*, the genus is *Theobroma*. There are 22 different species of *Theobroma*: the one we are interested in is *Theobroma cacao*. That's the easy bit. The Swedish botanist Linnaeus chose the name *Theobroma cacao* in his 1753 taxonomy because he wanted to call cacao the 'food (*-broma*) of the gods (*theo-*)'. The fascinating – if confusing – factor is that there are many varieties and sub-species of cacao in the world, giving rise to many flavours.

As *T. cacao* travelled to different regions, different types developed and adapted to their sites and climates – what the wine business prizes highly as terroir. Fans of single-origin chocolate and bean-to-bar producers will want eventually to trace the details for themselves. For the present it's enough to be aware that there is great diversity, and this diversity must be protected.

Facing page: The volcanic islands of São Tomé and Príncipe lie on the Equator, and are a tropical paradise where cacao can flourish in a healthy, shady interplanting of diverse tree types.

Above: Cacao defies categorisation, as it forms hybrids so easily. These pods were picked up within a small area in the Democratic Republic of Congo by the Original Beans team.

There are three main names to learn when it comes to cacao: Criollo, Forastero and Trinitario.

Criollo (pronounced 'cree-oh-yo'; meaning 'native' or 'local', like 'Creole'). Originated in Central America and now also found in parts of the Caribbean as well as Madagascar and Sri Lanka. The ripe pods are soft, deeply ridged, a sumptuous red or orange colour. The beans inside are pale pink or white – hence the name of the distinctly pale Porcelana Criollo. Low-yielding and rare (between 1 and 5 per cent of global production), it is highly prized for its flavours and lack of bitterness and it is slowly being introduced to plantations around the world. Like Trinitario (below), Criollo is known in the industry as a 'fine or flavour' bean. Versions include the beans of Venezuela's famed origin, Chuao (pronounced 'ch-wow').

Forastero (meaning 'foreigner'). Originated in the Amazon River basin. Looked down upon by chocolate purists, but essential to chocolate eaters because it accounts for the majority of cocoa beans harvested (around 85 per cent). Hardy, with higher yields than Criollo, it is a more economic crop, although the flavour is more bitter and less delicate. The pods are large, hard even when ripe, and green or yellow in colour, with dark purple beans. The main types are the Amelonado and the well-flavoured Nacional, or Arriba, of Ecuador. Widespread across Africa, Asia and Brazil.

Trinitario is a hybrid of Criollo and Forastero, developed in the 18th century on Trinidad (hence its name), but it is now grown outside the island. The ripe pods are hard and typically purple-coloured, with dark and light beans. Highly rated for its flavour.

There are a number of other types related to specific origins that are rated by chocolatiers, such as Ocumare from Venezuela and Esmeralda from Ecuador.

AN EQUATORIAL HARVEST

It's humid and shady in the plantation. Underfoot there's a soft, steamy mulch of fallen leaves and undergrowth. The evergreen cacao trees flourish at 65–70 per cent humidity – they need at least 100cm (40in) of rain a year, spread throughout the year. They need average temperatures between 20° and 36°C (68° and 97°F). Too windy, too sunny, soil too acid – all of these put the crop at risk. The trees are also vulnerable to pests and diseases.

Above: On the island of Príncipe, off the coast of West Africa: planting cacao, keeping the ground tidy and managing the shade.

The cacao tree begins to produce at five years old, and becomes really fruitful at 10–15 years. The trees may grow up to 8m (26ft) or more. Cacao flourishes in shade, though some commercial plantations manage to grow their cacao in full sun. In the most natural situations, cacao is overplanted by other trees: in this way its growth is controlled, the trees are closer to the ground and therefore easier to manage, and the cover trees protect the fruit from storm and wind.

Growing cacao is a lengthy, low-profit business. Each pod takes up to six months to reach maturity, and weighs between 200g (7oz) and 1kg (2lb 4oz). The ripe fruits do not drop off the tree, which only enhances cacao's mysterious qualities. Cacao alone of the trees needs vertebrate animals – monkeys, bats, rats, squirrels, humans – to detach the pods from the trunk.

A commercial plantation has two harvests a year; depending on the region, the main crop runs from October to December, with another from May to July, so the trees are alive with delicate white orchid-like flowers. Cacao's distinguishing feature is that the flowers and the pods grow directly from the trunk – surely it is endowed with marvellous properties. The mystery is that despite the abundance of flowers, very few pods are formed: on average, just 30 per tree. Midges, the minutely munching bane of any humid climate, are the key to successful pollination.

Above: On the Åkesson estate in Madagascar, the red Criollos (left) and the multicoloured Trinitarios (right) are ready for cleaning. The yellow spines on the pods indicate ripeness.

As the pods do not all ripen at the same time, the trees need to be visited and revisited over a period of a month. Each pod is sliced off with a machete and it is skilled work avoiding damage to both tree and pod. The beans are cracked open with a wooden club or a machete, again with care to avoid damage to the precious beans. There are few shortcuts to growing quality cacao.

Inside the pod there are 30 to 40 beans nestling in a succulent white pulp. Textbooks describe the pulp as mucilaginous. If you ever get the chance, try it – it is deliciously sweet, with a mild exotic flavour like lychee. Some regions in

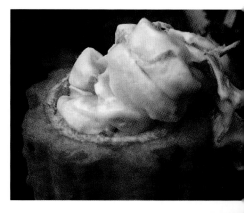

the Americas still make a drink from the pulp in preference to drinking chocolate. It is important to enjoy the pulp fresh, as it oxidises and spoils quickly. Pop a pulp-covered bean fresh from the pod in your mouth and it's like sucking a large lychee stone with the same milky flesh. But the pleasure all too quickly disappears, as the bean's bitter, tannic note comes through. This is the cycle of cacao: animals ate the delicious pulp, spitting out the seeds and scattering them as they went.

Above: Pick out one of the beans in its juicy coat and pop it in your mouth. The fruity white flesh is delicious! Just remember to spit out the bitter unfermented cacao bean inside.

Above: These beans in Virunga, in the Democratic Republic of Congo, are fermenting indoors in a box lined with banana leaves. The ambient temperature is about 30°C (86°F), and it takes three to four days to complete the fermentation process.

THE TRANSFORMATION BEGINS

There are 19 steps to the production of chocolate from bean to bar, says Philipp Kauffmann, conservationist and joint owner of Original Beans (see page 176). Whether the producer takes the artisan route or a more industrial one, the processes are broadly similar, though the technology may be different.

Fermentation To begin with, the beans, still coated with pulp, are piled on the ground on sheets of banana leaves and covered with more leaves or piled up in boxes. Left in the heat, the sweet pulp begins to ferment, breaking the sugar into glucose and fructose, and turning some of the protein into free amino acids and peptides. It is this process that creates the flavour precursors. Fermentation is fundamental – chocolate cannot be made without it. The care taken here makes the difference between a good bar and a great one. The pulp turns to acetic acid and evaporates. The beans change in colour and flavour, the fermentation soothing their bitterness. Taste with a producer and he or she will point out the faults and off-flavours from poor fermentation.

Drying The fermented beans are then spread out and left to dry evenly, turning into the sumptuous brown colour that suggests the promise of chocolate. In a tropical climate there's inevitably a risk of rain to spoil the drying, so growers have to be ready to cover the beans. Despite this, the traditional way of drying in the open, with regular raking, is best because it avoids the risk of taint from wood or fuel. The beans must lose almost all their moisture – leaving just 6 per cent – and half their weight. The average tree therefore yields just 500g–1kg (1lb 2oz–2lb 4oz) of dried beans. For growers paid by weight there is a temptation to leave more moisture in the beans to make them heavier. A good chocolate producer has to have strict controls on quality here and down the chain. A good grower will know accurately by feel whether the cacao has lost the correct amount of moisture. The dry, stable cacao is now ready for shipping, whether in traditional sacks or in more reliable inert containers. At this point the crop becomes a commodity, traded on international markets in the same way as coffee or sugar. Only a tiny percentage of cacao is processed in the country of origin by a plantation owner or a co-operative. Cacao is a tropical crop; chocolate is still a manufactured product of the temperate world.

CHOCOLATE PRODUCTION TODAY

Today the world produces around 3.5 million tonnes (3.8 million tons) of cacao per year. Seventy per cent of that comes from West Africa (from the Côte d'Ivoire and Ghana in particular). The urgent issue today is the threat to the rainforest and to the tropical climates on which cacao depends. Experts predict that there will no cacao left in Ghana – one of the powerhouses of cacao for confectionery – in 25 years time. Effectively, as the world gets warmer, Ghana will simply become too hot for cacao to germinate. Ghana has one of the

Above: It is not just the colour that changes as the cacao beans are dried – the flavours are developing, too. Regular turning of the beans is necessary for an even result.

highest deforestation rates in the world, at 1.9 per cent per year, as farmers turn to other, more profitable crops. As the forests disappear, so the rainfall reduces. Rivers and streams dry up. The Sahel transitional desert zone has been moving south, and viruses are taking their toll, too. Cacao benefits from a complex interplay of plants and insects, and in particular it needs midges to pollinate the flowers. All these are at risk as Ghana changes – and Ghana is not alone.

The bitter truth is that over half of the cacao farmers in West Africa live below the UN poverty line of US$2 a day. Two million cacao-farming families are trapped in a cycle of low production on small plots of land producing economically unsustainable annual yields of 250 to 400kg/hectare of beans, when in Malaysia the average yield is 1 tonne/hectare. However, Malaysian farmers, who came from nowhere in 1989 to being one of the world's top cacao producers in terms of volume 20 years later, are now choosing to move into palm oil production, which is a much more profitable crop.

What can be done? There is work happening on a number of fronts, much of it reasonably straightforward. Productivity can be increased. To achieve this means introducing better, more disease-resistant hybrids, as well as better managed holdings. The new cacao industry in Vietnam is small and in its infancy, but already looks to have both the quality and the yields. It was introduced by the French in 1898 but was blighted during the Vietnam War. Today in some areas yields are approaching 2 tonnes/hectare, making cacao sustainable.

Disease is a real threat to all growers. Brazil was once one of the world's leading producers, but was devastated in the 1980s when witches' broom, a fungal disease, swept through the plantations, killing the trees. Nevertheless, good farming practices and good plant material can go a long way towards preventing disease. Latin America grafts new plants onto old rootstocks, which means changes can be made more quickly to genetic material. In West Africa this practice is rare. At present most small farmers supply their own seeds, and therefore do not have the chance to improve their plant material. Teaching farmers about producing higher quality beans from better managed, more fertile soils, and introducing them to better farming practices, is essential. At present, say representatives of the Source Trust – an organisation dedicated to promoting sustainable and traceable farming practices to improve the livelihoods of farmers – just 15 per cent of the trees in Ghana produce 80 per cent of the crop.

The good news is that strategies are being discussed to implement sustainable farming. Yet at international level the wheels grind extremely slowly, and governments in cacao countries often impede progress. It is no wonder that individual conservation-minded pioneers are taking on the task themselves.

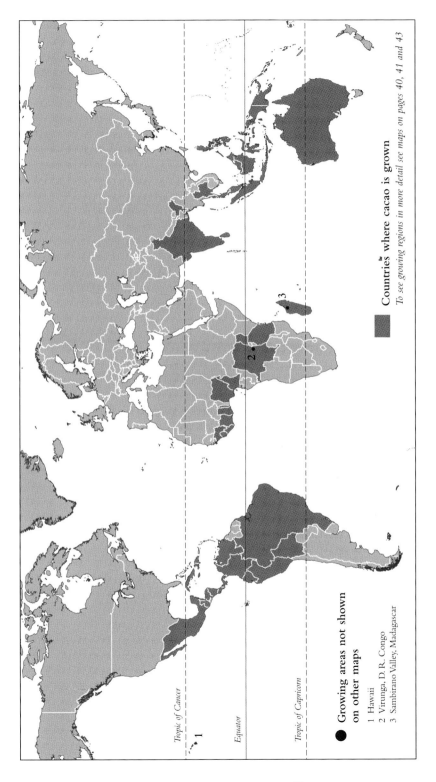

Countries where cacao is grown

To see growing regions in more detail see maps on pages 40, 41 and 43

Tropic of Cancer

Equator

Tropic of Capricorn

● Growing areas not shown
on other maps

1 Hawaii
2 Virunga, D. R. Congo
3 Sambirano Valley, Madagascar

The Americas and the Caribbean

■ Principal growing areas

Origins

1   Río Caribe
2   Barlovento
3   Chuao
4   Puerto Cabello
5   Sur del Lago
6   Santander
7   Las Esmeraldas
8   Napo
9   Alto Beni
10 Bahia

They are united in their determination to bring the growers into the loop, to make them proud of their work, and to give them an understanding of their role in the long chain of chocolate production.

ETHICAL EATING

Unwrapping a chocolate bar provides a little luxury. Discerning chocolate lovers increasingly focus on the producers, and their different styles and techniques. Less glamorous but a good deal more significant are the growers.

Fair trade is intended to create a fairer distribution of the profits of global commodities, such as cocoa and coffee. It is an important consideration, for the whole edifice of chocolate was built on foundations that were anything but fair. The native Americans were decimated by the arrival of the Europeans. If the conquistadores did not kill them in the bloodshed of the conquest, then the dysentery and smallpox that they and their successors brought with them certainly did. It has been estimated that as many as eight million died.

After disease came slavery. Workers were needed in the plantations to meet European demand for cacao and sugar, so slaves were imported from Africa, in the triangular trade that also exported cocoa and sugar to Europe, and weapons from Europe to Africa. Slavery was outlawed in Europe in the 1840s, yet this did not bring an end to slavery in cacao production. The most powerful recent work on cocoa and slavery is Carol Off's *Bitter Chocolate*, a distressing record of the trafficking of children to the Côte d'Ivoire, and also a chilling contemporary tale of corruption and exploitation in West Africa. It prompts every chocolate eater to demand to know more about their indulgence: its origin, and under what conditions it was grown and harvested.

Fairtrade, established in the late 1980s, took the first steps in educating consumers about these issues, and gave them some confidence about the sourcing of the products. Fairtrade is an independent body that works in partnership with producers in developing countries. It ensures that farmers receive the guaranteed minimum or world market price (whichever is higher), plus the Fairtrade premium of US$150 per tonne. This premium can be used to improve health and educational facilities, and to teach growers about how to create a better product and understand their role in the chocolate business.

The first Fairtrade label was Max Havelaar, launched in Holland in the 1980s and replicated in other markets across Europe and North America. In the United Kingdom, chocolate blazed the Fairtrade trail. Green & Black's **Maya Gold** (see page 128), made from cacao from Belize, was certified in 1994. In 2009 the leviathan Cadbury Schweppes announced that it was turning over the production of its leading brand, Dairy Milk, to Fairtrade in the United Kingdom and Ireland. This may be happening in only two countries initially, but the effect of this in Ghana is significant, as it triples the sales of that country's Fairtrade cocoa, and where one company begins others will follow. For the Fairtrade movement this is an important moment, though it threatens the smaller Fairtrade-only brands on sale in the United Kingdom and Ireland.

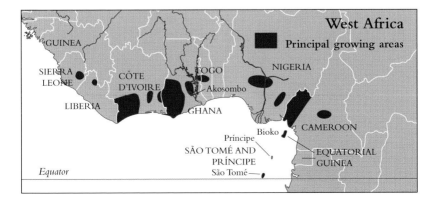

FAIRTRADE OR FAIR TRADE?

The proportion of the world's chocolate manufacturers signing up to Fairtrade remains small. Some producers have strong opinions about why they prefer not to join up. They argue that there is too much bureaucracy for growers to handle. Some suggest that the Fairtrade system puts the funding and the decisions about where to spend it into the hands of the wrong local people. There is a strong argument that the system maintains the status quo, rather than supporting different approaches to the market. In addition, some claim it damages the growers who are not part of fair-trade systems. Before you buy a bar, read the wrapper and ask yourself what, if anything, the producer of the chocolate in your hands has done to support and reward its workers and their families.

A growing number of small chocolate producers prefer to work directly with growers and develop their own models of a sustainable relationship. They pay more than the market rate for cacao, and in addition support the communities. Amedei (see page 70), Askinosie (see page 78), Kaoka (see page 146) and Original Beans (see page 178) are case studies in bean-to-bar production.

A SUSTAINABLE FUTURE

In an ideal world, a cacao plantation is a model of sustainable working. The healthy cacao tree flourishes with interplanting, with shady crop-bearing trees protecting the cacao and giving the grower multiple potential for return on his crops. Yet cacao is a commodity that is stockpiled and traded far away with prices that can be manipulated and deny the farmers a sustainable income.

Chocolate is a delicious luxury in the developed world, but 'cacao is a poor

Left: Planting new trees in Piura, Peru. It generally takes three years to the first harvest.

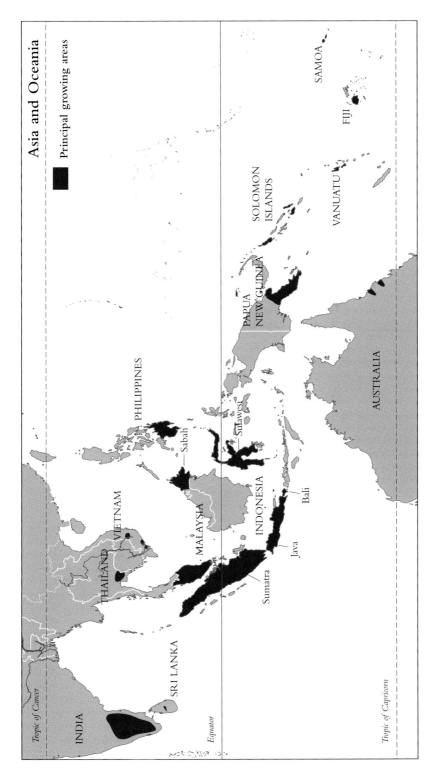

Asia and Oceania

■ Principal growing areas

Tropic of Cancer

INDIA

SRI LANKA

THAILAND

VIETNAM

PHILIPPINES

MALAYSIA

Sabah

Sulawesi

INDONESIA

Sumatra

Java

Bali

Equator

PAPUA NEW GUINEA

SOLOMON ISLANDS

VANUATU

SAMOA

FIJI

AUSTRALIA

Tropic of Capricorn

Leading producers of cacao

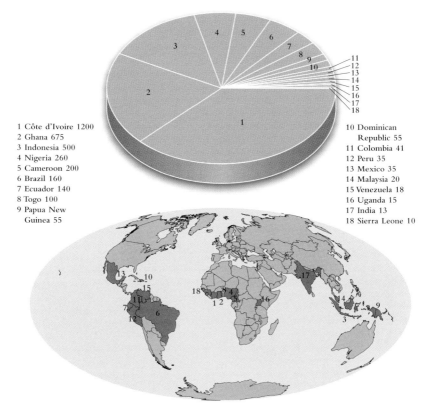

1 Côte d'Ivoire 1200
2 Ghana 675
3 Indonesia 500
4 Nigeria 260
5 Cameroon 200
6 Brazil 160
7 Ecuador 140
8 Togo 100
9 Papua New
   Guinea 55

10 Dominican
    Republic 55
11 Colombia 41
12 Peru 35
13 Mexico 35
14 Malaysia 20
15 Venezuela 18
16 Uganda 15
17 India 13
18 Sierra Leone 10

Note Estimates in thousand metric tonnes 2009–10. Source: International Cocoa Organization. Total for Togo is somewhat inflated due to substantial tonnages being imported from neighbouring countries. Other countries produce less than 10,000 tonnes per annum.

Cacao in a nutshell (or a pod...)

As the chart above shows, just two countries, Côte d'Ivoire and Ghana, next-door neighbours in West Africa, produce around half the world's cacao. In all, Africa produces 70 per cent of the world's cacao. Next come Asia and Oceania, followed by the Americas.

In terms of chocolate, consumption is growing. First, there are new markets to explore. Secondly, there is an increasing demand for chocolate with notably higher cocoa content – hence the focus of this book on 70% bars.

Curiously, we are consuming more cacao than is produced. How can this be? Easy – cacao is one of those commodities that is traded on international exchanges in virtual and actual amounts. When stored at the right temperature and humidity cacao can last for several years, just right for an investor to play the market – even if the grower is short-changed.

man's crop', a senior official from the cacao industry told me. He added, 'We may have better hybrids and pesticides, but effectively we are still farming as we did 100 years ago.' That is why some producers see their role as fundamentally restructuring local economies. One of the owners of Original Beans (see page 176) came into cacao from a previous career in rainforest conservation: 'we don't think of ourselves as a chocolate company; we are a conservation company, and we are here for the long term.' Working outside Fairtrade, 'we have the opportunity to redesign the supply chain. It is a unique opportunity to go from the vicious circle of deforestation/exploitation of labour/making a poor chocolate to the virtuous one of preserving the habitats and producing good chocolate.' Part of this includes introducing time-saving technologies, from bicycles (see below) to GPS.

Most of the chocolate makers featured in the Chocolate Directory in this book choose not to be involved in the farming of cacao. A small but growing band of pioneers is selecting beans and handling all the production. Others enter the process part-way through, starting with cocoa solids or cocoa liquor, the partly processed cocoa from one of the major producers. The remainder prefer to start their journey into fine bars with finished chocolate. Is there an opportunity in the coming years for growers in the countries of origin to build a parallel market to the international processors of cacao and to strengthen themselves against the manipulations of the market?

Above: In the Democratic Republic of Congo, bicycles from the Wheels4Life charity help growers transport their sacks of cocoa beans.

FROM CACAO TO CHOCOLATE

The Netherlands and the United States are the two most likely first destinations for the bulk of cacao beans. They need careful processing before they become a chocolate bar. Cleaning is the first step, to remove leaves, twigs and general detritus; this can be done mechanically. The beans are then ready to be roasted.

Roasting The beans are roasted in a cylindrical roaster and the shells become brittle. It is at this stage that the manufacturer can enhance the character of the beans, or alternatively ruin them completely. Temperature control is absolutely critical. Up until this point there are many similarities between coffee and cacao. The difference is that the coffee bean is ready to use after roasting. The cacao bean still has a long path to follow. That's why, as one US producer pointed out to me, there are hundreds of members of the Specialty Coffee Association: 'All they need is a roaster. Have you ever noticed how few people in the US make chocolate from beans? There are less than ten of them. Look at the convoluted steps and you can see why. You have to be mad.'

Grinding Once cooled, the shells are cracked. The husks are removed in a winnowing machine to reveal the nibs inside. These are ground in the melangeur (right) to form a paste, which is known as cocoa mass or liquor (not to be confused with alcoholic liquor). At this stage the chocolate contains just over 50 per cent cocoa butter. This is the stage when manufacturers can choose to press and separate the cocoa mass into its constituent cocoa butter and cocoa powder.

What's the fuss about lecithin?

One ingredient that gets the fine chocolate folk talking is lecithin. Lecithin is an emulsifier, helping to coat the cocoa particles in cocoa butter and contributing to the smooth, supple feel of the melt. It is also a money-saver, as it enables producers to use less of the more expensive cocoa butter. It is usually derived from soya, and most soya produced today is genetically modified. Intensive soya bean planting is one of the drivers of the destruction of the rainforests, the home of cacao. As it is extremely difficult to guarantee that soya is not genetically modified, producers concerned about the origins of their chocolate think it better to omit it altogether. Lecithin-free chocolate can be technically harder to handle, yet when finely made it is another sign of the chocolatier's expertise. Bill McCarrick of Sir Hans Sloane (see page 204) has another strong reason for omitting it: 'Have you ever tasted it? It's like wallpaper paste. Would you want that in your chocolate?'

Above: The roaster of the beans (left, in Grenada) needs a good sense of smell. The aim is to elicit warm chocolate flavours and aromas, not burnt ones. In the melangeur (right), the nibs, with sugar, are ground to a liquor between the granite rollers and the revolving granite slab.

Mixing The cocoa mass is mixed with – if used – sugar, milk, vanilla and soya lecithin. Manufacturers of mass-produced confectionery chocolate in the EU are also permitted to add up to 5 per cent of vegetable fats, but no fine chocolate producer does this. How does a chocolate maker decide whether to make a 35% or a 42% or 68% chocolate? Experience with the beans goes a long way, but simply making a small mix in a bowl will give a good idea. With the actual blend made, the crucial step is to refine the dough by passing it through rollers to reduce the particle size to 20 microns or even less. At the end of the process the chocolate is smooth, but this is not enough to create a finished product.

Conching The long process of mixing, stirring and aerating the liquid chocolate is the next step in refining its texture and flavour. The prime purpose of conching is to further reduce the particle size, and to coat each particle with cocoa butter. An added benefit is that various unwelcome flavours are also lost: for instance, acetic acid evaporates. During conching the flavours change and the sugars caramelise, assisting the development of baked flavours that is commonly found in Belgian and Swiss chocolate. Producers have to decide when is the best time to stop conching. Since chocolate has several hundred different flavour compounds, this is a matter of some skill.

Some producers have taken to putting the conch time on the wrapper. A higher number does not necessarily indicate a better chocolate; three days is not necessarily better than 40 hours. Austrian producer Zotter (see page 226) packs bars in pairs, making it possible to compare different conch times. There is a recent fashion to reduce times, in order to allow bolder expressions of flavour. The texture will be coarser but, says Bill McCarrick of Sir Hans Sloane (see page 204), 'it means your mouth finishes the conching'.

Tempering This is the final stage before shaping the chocolate into bars or using it for coating fillings. It is essential for the perfect sheen and the stability of the chocolate. Liquid chocolate, ready to shape and solidify, was off-puttingly described to me by a poet of the industry as 'an intimate mixture of solid particles suspended in fat'. He commented that the key to understanding chocolate was that cocoa butter was polymorphic: it has four different melting points between 18°C (64.4°F) and 34.4°C (93.9°F). This degree of accuracy explains why many producers prefer to leave tempering to an expert: the experts do it so often that they do not need thermometers – visual appearance and feel is gauge enough.

The aim of tempering is to create a large number of small cocoa butter crystals in the most stable form. It is the small size and regular alignment of the crystals that makes a well-tempered bar shiny in appearance and smooth in the mouth.

When hand tempering the chocolatier pours out a pool of chocolate onto a marble slab, which will assist the cooling. As the chocolate cools from the edges in, the chocolatier lifts and smoothes the cooler chocolate towards the still warm, still liquid centre. As the most stable of the fat crystals starts to crystallise as it cools, the others will 'seed' around it. If they do not, white smears may appear, tell-tale signs that some of the fats have separated out. Tempering may look flamboyant, but it is a rapid process, requiring dexterity and full concentration. As with pastry making, the essence is cool hands, grace and accuracy.

Creating the bar The last step is to pour the tempered chocolate into the chosen mould. The mould needs a firm hand, as it is important to shake out air bubbles. To encourage the set, the moulds are placed in a cooling tunnel. Alternatively, the tempered chocolate can be kept stable in a liquid form; in this form it can be transported to manufacturers. The tanker that just drove past on the motorway could be full of liquid chocolate.

Right: From tree to bar at The Grenada Chocolate Company. Top row, left to right: picking and drying in the open air. Second row, left to right: sorting the beans; adding sugar to the nibs for mixing in the melangeur; pouring the finished, tempered chocolate into moulds. Bottom row, left to right: the bars are wrapped by hand before shipping.

TASTING CHOCOLATE

D espite chocolate's global appeal, we do have different national tastes. One of the unexpected legacies of past empires is a taste for the coloniser's chocolate. This explains the dominance of Cadbury's Dairy Milk in some far-flung parts of the former British Empire in preference to Hershey's. This is particularly the case with milk chocolate, which is usually the style that we encounter first and which dominates our preferences for milk chocolate as adults. Even within Europe there remain bold contrasts among the key chocolate-producing and -consuming countries.

Spain continues to enjoy drinking chocolate, almost 500 years after the drink was introduced to the royal court. This is not a thin liquid, like a chocolate version of instant coffee with milk; Spain's is a sumptuous glossy drink that one could practically stand a spoon up in. In weekly markets and local festivities, stalls serve cups of unctuously thick chocolate accompanied by *churros* (deep-fried fritters) for dipping. In recent decades Spain has also developed a stylish approach to chocolate, influenced by the radicalism of its award-winning chefs, both the molecular gastronomers and the more orthodox.

For the French, dark chocolate has always had an elegant appeal. France has a strong tradition of patisserie, in which artisans used fine chocolate for their creations. Typically, French filled chocolates are small pieces, and the flavours are subtle. Until very recently, French chocolate was unchallenged as the best.

The Belgians undoubtedly have a sweet tooth, with an emphasis on dairy; local consumers prefer fillings based on cream and butter. The chocolate itself has a baked brownie character. White chocolate figures strongly in the selections, which are also very sugary. Belgium's chocolate companies were very successful at building an image as purveyors of accessible luxury, hence their presence at airport shops round the world. Nevertheless Belgian chocolate could not be described as cutting edge, although there are today individual chocolatiers in the country producing very fine chocolates.

Switzerland is renowned for its milk chocolate, and remains loyal to a rich, caramelised style which has been echoed over the Alps by some Italian producers. Italy is the home of *gianduja*, the hazelnut chocolate paste that in its most commercial form is sold as Nutella. A fine *gianduja*-filled chocolate is rich without excessive sweetness. Over in Germany there are significant producers, most of which started as small family-run patissiers. Their style is classic, but despite (or perhaps because of) the size of the country there is not a strictly identifiable typical 'German' flavour.

The British have long been milk chocolate fans, although in a style that the rest of Europe views as distinctly un-chocolatey. Historically, British dark chocolate was sweet and not particularly dark. No wonder, with the arrival of fine chocolatiers, Britain is at last becoming such a lively market for fine dark chocolate. Scandinavia shows parallels with Britain, in its relatively recent arrival to fine chocolate appreciation. Sweden is currently the most dynamic Scandinavian country, with several new chocolatiers springing up.

The United States, like the United Kingdom, is a divided nation. The taste for the historic producers remains. However, there is an outburst of artisans, sourcing beans or developing experimental fillings. Australia has followed a similar route, and today is enjoying the work of artisans interested in origins.

Japan has a serious interest in fine chocolate, and a respect for fine producers. China remains a small market. Whichever of the big brands comes to the marketplace first will lead the national taste, at least at the outset.

FLAVOURS OF THE WORLD

As with wine, beans from different parts of the world have different flavours and characteristics. But as with wine, how the chocolate is made is just as important as where it comes from. It is not always easy to identify the origin of the bean. The processing makes all the difference. Two producers using the same beans may come up with two very different chocolates. There may be similarities in acidity and intensity, but a poor fermentation or a harsh roast can spoil a fine chocolate. Beans that have been dried over wood fires may have a smoky bacon aroma; beans stored in a damp sack will be tainted with an earthy character.

While some producers focus on getting the best from beans from a single origin, others pride themselves on their skill in blending beans from two or more countries, or even from one or more growers in the same origin. Generalising about flavour profiles of different producing countries is a difficult and contentious business. However, if you choose a single-origin bar, then these are some of the broad flavour characteristics you may look for. The directory section of this book, beginning on page 62, is much more explicit about the flavours of origins as interepreted by individual producers.

Above: Beni, Bolivia: a magnificent wild cacao tree over 100 years old.

Above: One family, many types: contrast these Forastero pods from Madagascar with the Nacional pods from Peru, overleaf.

Bolivia Bolivian cacaos are distinguished by their spicy, woody notes, lifted by some red fruits.

Brazil Much of Brazil's production was wiped out by disease in the 1980s, and today it is a net importer of chocolate. Some of the cocoa butter has a lower melting point than that of other cacao, which means that it does not set easily, or 'snap'. Typically the style is honeyed, low in acidity, sometimes with a smoky character. However, some insiders say that this smokiness has nothing to do with terroir and has everything to do with wood smoke contamination from poorly handled drying.

Colombia Often produces chocolate with bright red fruit character.

Côte d'Ivoire A generally rounded chocolate character, which explains its attractiveness for mass production of chocolate.

Dominican Republic Trinitario beans produce a fine, delicate, aromatic chocolate. Substantial investment by the government has greatly improved quality in recent times, and the country is now a significant supplier of organically grown cacao.

Ecuador The chocolate is reputed to have a floral profile with blackcurrants and spice. The family tree of cacao here is complicated, as there have been many crossings over the years. A fine version of the Forastero, the Nacional, is known here; this is sometimes called Arriba Nacional, or just Arriba. It seems likely that 'Arriba' refers to the 'up' river origins where these distinctively floral notes are found. But there is also a type called CCN51, which has been much criticised for its drabness, and which has crossed with Arriba. However, as with other beans, much depends on the quality of the processing.

Ghana One chocolatier told me that the flavour of Ghana 'hits you like a freight train'. Certainly it is convincingly chocolatey and services global demand for chocolate.

Grenada Having survived the devastation of recent hurricanes, Grenada's cacao is back on stream (until the next one!). The style is lively and complex – boldly acidic, at times woody, at others red-fruited.

Indonesia Java is a very popular origin for milk chocolate because of its creamy, honeyed richness, the chocolate equivalent of a latte in coffee. Excellent cacao, partly as a result of expert growers. Mainly Criollo. Bali has a similar honeyed, raisin fruit character.

Jamaica Can be earthy and woody, but also reveals berry fruit notes. Very dependent on the quality of the harvest and handling.

Madagascar The Sambirano Valley on the north-west tip of Madagascar is a popular origin, for its biodiversity as much as for its fruitiness. The chocolate is relatively mild and full, often with a tangerine orange note.

Above: The fruity character of Madagascan cacao makes it a popular origin for chocolate lovers.

Above: Nacional pods in Piura, Peru: reforestation will bring new life to the region.

Malaysia The cacao from Malysia has notably low acidity, because it is grown within a narrow range of temperatures between day and night. Cacao benefits from the cool as well as the warmth, and grows best where there is a greater diurnal temperature difference.

Mexico A historic name in the story of cacao. Today, there are interesting projects reviving Criollo trees. Xoconusco was Montezuma's personal estate and some producers are starting to make Xoconusco bars. Samples so far show a woody, tannic character alongside some typical chocolate flavours.

Papua New Guinea These beans bring earthy, acidic, tobacco flavours to the chocolate, which can be smoothed and tamed by careful production and longer conching.

Peru Peru's profile tends towards the nutty and honeyed, with deep chocolate notes. There can be peppery, spicy undertones, too.

São Tomé and Príncipe This island chocolate risks being bold and bitter, but is soothed by some fruitiness. This is an origin that shows the difference the producer can make. Some producers tame the wildness, others let it loose.

St Lucia The crop has a good lively acidity, balancing the richness of the cacao.

Venezuela An iconic origin, where the finest Criollo beans are found. The Porcelana type found here is famed for its lack of bitterness. The name comes from their pale, porcelain colour, one that carries through to the chocolate itself, where the colour is notably lighter. Domori (see page 114) has a particularly delightful description of a Porcelana bar: 'It has notes of bread, butter and jam with an exalted smoothness.' I agree entirely, except for the bread, perhaps. There are several outstanding origins in Venezuela, notably Chuao, which is on the north coast and can be reached only by boat. As with other precious items, there appears to be more chocolate made from Chuao than there are beans produced. The Italian producer Amedei (see page 70) is currently closely associated with Chuao, but other producers also make Chuao chocolates. Chocolate is produced in a number of dangerous places in the world, and Venezuela is currently one of the most challenging in terms of personal safety for both growers and visiting producers alike.

Vietnam Still a relatively small producer, but the quality of the trees and the processing is promising.

Above: Cacao beans drying in front of the church at Chuao in Venezuela, chocolate's most famous origin. Note the precision of the drying circles.

HOW TO TASTE

This section explains how to taste chocolate like an expert. Many people find it difficult to approach chocolate rationally – not only because it is so delicious, but also because it has so many varied associations with pleasure. Yet tasting is a straightforward process that everyone can learn. The most important point is to be systematic: this allows you to compare every chocolate on an equal footing.

Before we start tasting, let's consider why it is both interesting and useful to take it seriously. First, tasting systematically makes eating chocolate even more enjoyable. Using all the senses – sight, hearing, touch, smell, taste – really enhances the pleasure. Second, it makes chocolate memorable. Just like remembering a tune and being able to sing it later, tasting carefully means it is possible to recall the flavours. This is particularly useful to people involved in the chocolate business, whether chefs or retailers, but can benefit everyone who buys chocolate. Third, regular tasting helps develop a vocabulary. Chocolate, like any specialist food or drink, has its own language. Being able to use the right words to express a fine difference between chocolates will increase your enjoyment, as you will be able to select flavours and styles with confidence. Look at the packaging: several producers include tasting notes, which may help you to distinguish flavours. Finally, having honed your tasting skills with something as pleasurable as chocolate, you can then transfer them – to wine, to cheese and to other fine foods.

The world of fine chocolate can be as intimidating as the world of fine wine. Learning to taste like the experts breaks down the barriers. Today's fine chocolatiers are keen to welcome new enthusiasts without preconceptions. There are two ways to taste: fast and slow.

To start with the fast: however keen to eat you are, this takes only a moment. There are three steps: **Look, Listen, Sniff. Look** – even a quick glance at the chocolate is revealing. **Listen** – for the snap as you break a square off the bar. Then **sniff** – savour the chocolate aromas. Now put it in your mouth, enjoying the character of the bar. However fast you look, listen and sniff, you must allow time for the melt. Let the chocolate release its flavours slowly.

The slow method may at first seem pretentious, and certainly it is best practised with other chocolate lovers, or by yourself. I learned the formal principles of tasting through wine tasting, and found that it is best to develop your skills in private (especially since wine tasting involves spitting). However, I also learned that even the fast method can uncover plenty of information, without making it obvious to outsiders that one is doing a geeky tasting in one's head.

The **slow method** covers six stages: **Appearance, Snap, Aroma, Texture, Flavour, Length.** Make a note of your personal opinion at each stage.

1. Appearance: Unwrapping a bar can be a theatrical moment. Take time to look at the wrapper, and consider the care that has gone into it. Set it aside to refer to later. Unwrap the whole bar and look at it front and back. Consider the shape and decoration of the bar. Is there an appealing sheen? Are there any air holes, signs of uneven handling, swirl marks on the underside? Or any sign of bloom? Consider the colour – different origins and beans will show different tones, as will different degrees of cocoa solids. *Notes: Shape, thickness, design; sheen (or lack of); faults (bloom, air holes); colour (ochre, brown, red-brown, purple-brown, mahogany)*

2. Snap: Break off a small square. Listen for a convincing snap or crack. This will vary with the thickness of the bar and the temperature, as well as with the type and quality of the fats used. A well-tempered dark bar should give a satisfying snap. *Notes: Clean, crisp, weak, dull*

3. Aroma: Hold the square close to your nose and give it a good sniff. Let it warm slightly between your fingers and then give another sniff. How intense is the aroma? Reflect on the aromas beyond the smell of chocolate. *Notes: Floral, fruity, wine, honeyed, creamy, nutty, spicy, toasty, smoky, earthy, animal, chemical*

4. Texture: Place a small piece of chocolate on your tongue. Let it melt slowly. This is the time when it is easy to be distracted, but it is important to concentrate. Think about the texture and the flavour simultaneously. How rapid or slow is the melt? How does the chocolate feel as it melts? Is there any texture, ranging from a lightly grainy character to coarseness? As the melt finishes, is there any grip of tannin on the gums, as there is with some red wines, or with stewed tea? Or is the overall effect silky? *Notes: Silky, smooth, uneven, grainy, sludgy, fudgy (note how the texture changes over time); melt (fast, medium, lingering); body (light, delicate, elegant, hollow, medium-bodied, full-bodied, bold); tannin (presence or absence; subtle, velvety, firm, bold, dominant, drying, astringent)*

5. Flavour: While thinking about the melt and texture, also monitor the development of flavour in your mouth. How does it begin? Does the flavour build slowly, boldly or not at all? What is the dominant flavour at the 'mid-palate' – after the beginning, but before the finish? Is there any sense of acidity or astringency – and does it stand apart or is it balanced by the other flavours? Assess the flavour profile dispassionately – it may not be to your taste, but is it successful? Finally is the finish, the last flavour in the mouth, clean? *Notes: Character (concentrated, complex, clean); bitterness; astringency; acidity; consider the balance between these three and the effect of sweetness, if any; full-bodied, hollow*

6. Length: How long does the flavour stay in your mouth after the chocolate has gone? Some producers claim their chocolates last for 30 minutes, so do not be in haste to taste too many samples too quickly. It is not necessary to sit for 30 minutes with a stopwatch, but it is enough to note whether the flavour disappeared quickly, or whether it persisted for a longer time. *Notes: Short, long, intense; elegant, powerful*

Take a final look at the wrapper. Does the date stamp confirm your perception of freshness (or of staleness)? Did you have any views on the ingredients? Are there any tasting notes on the wrapper? Do you agree with them? If you do, make a note if they extend your vocabulary. That is the tasting process. It takes many words to describe what is, in practice, a reasonably rapid procedure. Remember that there is no right answer. Just be fair, honest and consistent.

HOW THE TASTINGS WORK

The pages that follow contain profiles of 82 leading producers around the world. Some of these are 'bean-to-bar' producers, ranging from some who make finished bars in the area where the trees grow, to others who purchase beans from a range of suppliers. Other chocolatiers prefer to select fine chocolate from another producer, which they then temper and shape to their own style. Some companies featured here are famous as patissiers, for whom chocolate bars may be only a small part of the business. Many of the companies produce a range of bars – dark, milk, white, flavoured – and some of the outstanding bars are mentioned in the text.

For the tasting, one bar was chosen from each company. To make comparison as straightforward as possible this was a 70% cocoa solids bar (or as close to 70% as possible), either a house blend, or a single-origin bar representative of the house style. The tasting notes relate to this one bar. The profile below is the guide I use when tasting. It gives an impression of intensity and adds another dimension to the taste profiles on each page in the directory that follows.

SAMPLE PROFILE

Floral	𝓯𝓯𝓯		Nutty	𝓯
Fruity	𝓯		Spicy	𝓯
Winey	𝓯		Toasty	𝓯𝓯
Honey	𝓯		Smoky	𝓯
Creamy	𝓯𝓯𝓯		Earthy	𝓯

EXAMPLES OF FLAVOURS

Floral: jasmine, violet, rose, honeysuckle
Fruity: citrus acidity (lemon, orange, tangerine, lime, grapefruit), tropical fruits, passion fruit, banana, dried fruits
Winey: red fruit, redcurrant, balsamic
Honey: vanilla, fudge, syrup, treacle, biscuit
Creamy: coconut, milk, cream, caramel
Nutty: walnut, hazelnut, almond
Spicy: white pepper, black pepper, chilli, ginger, liquorice, cinnamon, nutmeg
Toasty: lightly roasted, high toast, burnt
Smoky: leather, tannin, ash, rubber, tar, meaty, tobacco
Earthy: woody, mushroomy

INTENSITY OF FLAVOURS

0 Not present	1 slight 𝓯	2 medium 𝓯𝓯	3 intense 𝓯𝓯𝓯

Tips for successful tasting

In an ideal world, there are a number of factors that will make tasting easier:

• Taste in the morning with a clear head
• Keep away from strong flavours such as coffee – and, of course, cigarettes
• Rinse your hands with water, but avoid scented soap. Perfumes and aftershaves are no-nos in tasting rooms
• Have pen and paper ready to take notes
• Taste in a cool, well-lit room, with good natural light. Taste from a white plate or paper. Keep track of which chocolate is which, as it is very easy to get bars mixed
• Have cool, still water to hand
• Some tasters recommend good white bread, and slivers of crisp apples, for cleansing the palate occasionally
• The ideal size for a chocolate tasting sample is 5g
• Have a container ready to collect the rubbish. Look at the wrapper before you discard it; sometimes it will have interesting facts and even tasting notes
• If you are tasting with friends, taste in silence first. An opinionated taster may influence others
• Respect your fellow tasters. There is no right answer when it comes to tasting. There may be technical faults, but for the rest all systematic assessments are valid
• For most tastings a selection of eight chocolates is ideal. For work purposes, 20 chocolates is seriously the maximum

Above: Chocolate tasting is fun! A small disc can tempt, charm – or dismay.

TWO

CHOCOLATE DIRECTORY

Åkesson's

As a Swede, Bertil Åkesson enjoys pointing out that it was another Swede, Carl Linnaeus (1707–78), who made such a significant contribution to chocolate by giving the plant its botanical name, *Theobroma cacao*. Bertil and his family encountered chocolate via the travels of Bertil's father, a diplomat who finally settled in Madagascar in the 1970s. The family's 2300-hectare (5680-acre) estate lies in the Sambirano Valley in north-west Madagascar and has been growing cacao – and aromatic peppers – since 1920.

After producing cacao for chocolate companies for seven years, Bertil had a precise idea of what chocolate from his plantation should taste like. He produced his first organic, single-plantation, 75% cocoa solids bar in 2009. In Madagascar, Åkesson's current production is 300 tonnes of Trinitario beans and a mere 2 tonnes of Criollo. The next project is to source Trinitario from Bali for a 75% bar, and for a 45% milk bar with Balinese Taksu salt. Åkesson has a joint venture at the Fazenda Sempre Firme estate in Bahia, Brazil, growing a Forastero variety called Parazinho. He says, 'I am in love with Brazil and their cocoa and I definitely want to promote it. Other companies have started to produce single-origin chocolate from Brazil, so there is a trend towards recognising the quality of the cocoa, even though it is mainly Forastero.'

Some of Åkesson's Madagascan bars are spiced with pepper grown on the estate. There is always a risk with pepper and chilli bars

NAME OF THE BAR *Åkesson's Single Plantation Chocolate*
COCOA SOLIDS, BLEND OR ORIGIN *75%, Madagascar,*
Ambolikapiky Plantation, Criollo; Organic
INGREDIENTS *Cocoa, cane sugar, cocoa butter, GMO-free soya lecithin*
WEIGHT OF BAR *60g* **BAR MADE** *France*
WEBSITE *www.akessons-organic.com*
AROMA *Chocolate with notes of rose petals and red apples*
TASTE *Complex and savoury. Begins slowly with restrained mineral notes, then builds through red fruit, treacle and a boom of spice with a promise of chilli, to a full-on savoury expression with leather and tannin. Finally soothed by a note of tangerine. Finish is long with a firm, tannic grip and a sense of salt.*

PROFILE

Floral	🍫		Nutty	🍫
Fruity	🍫🍫🍫		Spicy	🍫🍫
Winey	🍫🍫		Toasty	🍫
Honey	🍫		Smoky	🍫
Creamy	🍫🍫		Earthy	🍫🍫

that the spice will be far too strong, but Åkesson's have got it more or less right. The **Wild Voatsiperifery Pepper** has a delicate dominance, and makes a fine foil to the tannic, leathery finish of the chocolate. It is an excellent companion to an espresso. The **Black Pepper** is more punchy, but is soothed by a green apple character typical of Madagascan pepper, which gives a mouthwatering finish to the spicy mid-palate. Åkesson grinds the pepper in an 'old coffee mill' and keeps it in flakes rather than grinding it to a powder. There is a very fine crunch to the pepper, which adds a delicate texture.

Alter Eco

France's leading Fairtrade food brand is a business that wears its heart on its sleeve, ticking all the 21st-century boxes – organic and aiming to be zero carbon, it promises the 'highest guarantee of sustainable development'. If it hasn't quite got every environmentally friendly qualification, it wants to prove that it is trying hard. The inside cover of the card wrappers are full of information and photographs. It has even calculated the carbon footprint of each 100g bar: of the 273g of carbon generated, 108g are generated by manufacturing, 63g by transport, 62g by distribution and 40g by the consumer.

The chocolate is made in Switzerland and the ingredients list on the back label (see facing page) illustrates the travails of sourcing beans confronting today's producer, especially when aiming for organic or fair-trade certification. There's little chance of reflecting the terroir when the ingredients come from four different countries.

The range includes dark bars at 85%, 73%, 60% (see profile) and a milk bar at 43%, as well as bars flavoured with coffee, orange, mint and almonds. The most interesting flavoured bar is the 60% **Noir Quinoa** bar, with the strap line '*Osons, Croquons!*'[Be brave, let's crunch!]. A blend of puffed rice and South America's high-protein grain, it's different. If anything, though, the crunchy ingredients only emphasise the tannic grip of the chocolate.

Facing page: Cacao beans drying in the sun at Alter Eco's Peruvian supplier, the Acopagro co-operative in Peru. The beans need to be regularly raked for even drying, and covered if it rains.

NAME OF THE BAR *Alter Eco Noir Intense Force Brute*
COCOA SOLIDS, BLEND OR ORIGIN *60%;*
Fairtrade, organic, 'Objectif Zéro Carbone'
INGREDIENTS *Cocoa mass (Peru), raw cane sugar (Paraguay), cocoa butter (Dominican Republic), vanilla extract (Madagascar)*
WEIGHT OF BAR *100g* **BAR MADE** *Switzerland*
WEBSITE *www.altereco.com*
AROMA *Bright and fruity, with notes of hazelnut and toast*
TASTE *Overall zesty, citrussy impression. Starts with notes of lemon and rose, builds to a fudgy, caramel mid-palate, showing the influence of the sugar, with a bright citric finish.*

PROFILE

Floral	🌸🌸	Nutty	
Fruity	🌸🌸	Spicy	
Winey		Toasty	🌸
Honey	🌸🌸🌸	Smoky	🌸
Creamy	🌸🌸	Earthy	🌸

Amano

Amano's Art Pollard is one of the bright stars in the recent revival of fine chocolate in the United States. Most chocolate fans are content simply to enjoy eating chocolate. Not Art. So keen was he to find better chocolate that he decided to make his own. Fortunately he had a background in science, so after much trial and error, visits to European producers and a decade of tasting and testing, Amano was launched in 2006. The skill of the scientist-turned-engineer-turned-creative chocolatier shows in the silky melt and fine texture of the bars.

The factory is 64 km (40 miles) south of Salt Lake City, Utah. At 1454m (4770ft) above sea level, Amano is among the world's highest chocolate factories, in a dry and arid zone. 'At this altitude', says Pollard, 'the volatiles and acetic acid vaporise at a lower temperature, enhancing the flavour profile.' Pollard's interest is the complexity of the chocolate itself, which is why there are as yet no flavoured or spiced bars.

For the dark bars, all at 70%, Amano sources beans from many origins: Madagascar, the Dominican Republic, Venezuela, Ecuador and Bali. There are two 30% milk bars: **Ocumare** from Venezuela and **Jembrana** from Bali.

NAME OF THE BAR *Amano Artisan Chocolate Madagascar 70%*
COCOA SOLIDS, BLEND OR ORIGIN *70%, Sambirano Valley, Madagascar*
INGREDIENTS *Cocoa beans, raw cane sugar, cocoa butter, whole vanilla beans*
WEIGHT OF BAR *56g* **BAR MADE** *Orem, Utah, USA*
WEBSITE *www.amanochocolate.com*
AROMA *Bold: leafy, herbal, floral*
TASTE *A bright, sunshine lift of tangerine ripens to a broad, full richness, and a pure undertow of citrus. Slow to melt, with a fine-grained texture. The memory of citrus freshness persists; mocha develops on the finish. In all, a fine, mildly chocolatey impression.*

PROFILE

Floral	🌶🌶	Nutty	🌶
Fruity	🌶🌶🌶	Spicy	🌶
Winey	🌶	Toasty	
Honey	🌶	Smoky	
Creamy	🌶	Earthy	🌶

Amano's milk chocolate bars are subtle and smooth but my preference is for a milk bar that is darker than 30%. Pollard stresses that 'it is a hard balance to make a good "dark milk". My personal taste is toward the dark side but I have noticed that dark milk bars tend to be "not-quite-so-great" dark bars rather than "this-is-exceptionally-good" milk bars. It's not that they are bad, it's just that they are not as good as a dark bar made with the same beans. Thus there is a need for more milkiness so that they balance out.'

Amedei

Brother and sister Alessio and Cecilia Tessieri make chocolate in what must be one of the prettiest factory buildings in the world – its frontage is bright with reds, ochres and purples, a painting of a mass of ripe cacao trees and pods.

The Tessieris started up in the small town of Pontedera near Pisa in the early 1980s. Alessio (the more outgoing one) had gained business experience in the family's pastry distribution company, while Cecilia (the shy one) trained as a chocolatier in France. Both of them were focused on quality. The search for quality took Alessio to Venezuela where, like all bean-to-bar producers, he had to build trust and close relationships with farmers to be able to acquire the finest beans. In 2003, he gained access to cacao from Chuao, the iconic Criollo plantation close to the Caribbean Sea, and he retains a substantial investment there. Chuao creates chocolate of great delicacy, remarkably complex, with a red wine acidity and a note of baked plums.

Amedei quickly won an international reputation for its bars. **Chuao** is from the famed Chuao plantation. **Porcelana**, a bar of refined elegance, is made from porcelain-coloured Criollo beans from Venezuela, and has a seductively rich note of almonds, honey, caramel and a lift of tangerine. Amedei also makes a range of bars called **I Cru**, from individual plantations in Venezuela, Trinidad, Madagascar, Ecuador, Jamaica and Grenada; the packs include short, clear tasting notes – a good start for anyone wishing to distinguish the characteristics of the different origins.

Despite the fashion for single origins, Cecilia Tessieri is a master at blending. Her blends at 63%, 66% and 70%

NAME OF THE BAR *Amedei Toscano Black Cioccolato Fondente Extra 70%*
COCOA SOLIDS, BLEND OR ORIGIN *70%, blend of Trinitario and Criollo*
INGREDIENTS *Cocoa mass, cane sugar, cocoa butter, vanilla*
WEIGHT OF BAR *50g*
BAR MADE *Pontedera, Pisa, Tuscany, Italy*
WEBSITE *www.amedei.it*
AROMA *Warm chocolate aromas, with flowers and fruit*
TASTE *The very essence of chocolate. The start is delicate, offering a warm, rounded welcome of chocolate blended with an espresso coffee with a shot of foam. Clean, long finish.*

PROFILE

Floral	🌶🌶	Nutty	🌶
Fruity	🌶🌶	Spicy	
Winey	🌶🌶	Toasty	🌶🌶
Honey	🌶🌶	Smoky	🌶🌶
Creamy	🌶🌶	Earthy	🌶

(above) are all classics and '9' is her most complex blend. She also makes fun, flavoured bars (including pistachio, hazelnut, and peach and apricot), and small pralines and ganaches in intense flavours (ginseng, rhubarb and liquorice).

In the factory, the fine, melting texture for which Amedei is renowned is created by their well-worn conches. The result is a delicate chocolate with exceptional persistence. Try using a stopwatch to time how long the taste stays in your mouth!

The Tessieris' creation of Amedei is a remarkable achievement. With their complementary skills, the brother and sister team source fine cacaos and continue consistently to transform them into even finer chocolate.

Amma

Once upon a time, Brazil was the world's second largest exporter of cacao. Then, in 1989, the destructive fungal disease witches' broom started to lay waste to plantations in Bahia, Brazil's largest cacao-growing area. The disease gets its name from the way clusters of dead leaves and twigs form on branches, looking just like little brooms. The devastation had a major social impact: it is estimated that 200,000 Brazilians lost their jobs as a result and a further one million were indirectly affected.

Slowly Brazil's cacao industry is coming back to life. One of the new personalities in the revival of fine chocolate is Frederick Schilling, who made his name as the founder of Dagoba (see page 106) in the United States. The story goes that plantation owner Diego Badaró sent him 100g of cacao from his estate in Bahia in 2007, and Schilling was so impressed by the quality of the beans that he flew out to meet him at his estate within the month.

Schilling has a strong interest in sustainability, and the AMMA project has been set up to continue those ideals. Badaró farms his estate organically. He grows his cacao in the traditional way, called *cabruca* in Brazil, whereby the shorter cacao trees are protected beneath taller trees in an integrated environment. There is a determination with this project to produce not just chocolate, but sustainable, well-made chocolate from good cacao.

The cacao used is, says Schilling, Pará-Parázinho-Maranã. It is a Forastero variety and is 'the original native endemic cacao strain of Brazil and creates a wonderful base chocolate flavour...We also use hybrids, such as Scavina, which

NAME OF THE BAR *Amma Chocolate 75%*

COCOA SOLIDS, BLEND OR ORIGIN *75%*

INGREDIENTS *Organic cocoa mass, organic sugar, pure organic cocoa butter*

WEIGHT OF BAR *80g*

BAR MADE *Bahia, Brazil*

WEBSITE *www.ammachocolate.com.br*

AROMA *Dense and chocolatey*

TASTE *Starts with bright highlights of red cherries with a persistent citrus note. Rounds out to a full, rich mocha flavour, finishing with a grip of tannin. Very long.*

PROFILE

Floral		Nutty	🌰🌰
Fruity	🌰🌰	Spicy	🌰
Winey	🌰	Toasty	🌰🌰
Honey	🌰🌰	Smoky	🌰🌰
Creamy	🌰	Earthy	🌰

provides fruitier and more complex nuances...But our key determining factor for the cacao, regardless of genetic makeup, is the flavour...I feel we have, in a very short time, achieved our goal of producing the finest chocolate in Brazil.'

The range, labelled with the co-ordinates of the estate, includes bars at 85%, 75% (see above), 60% and 50%, as well as milk bars at 45% and 35%.

Above: Cutting open the cacao pods on Diego Badaró's estate in Brazil.

Antica Dolceria Bonajuto

Some people visit Sicily for Mount Etna, others for its beaches or its ruins, and still others for its wines. However, chocolate lovers make a pilgrimage to the town of Modica in the south-eastern corner of the island for its connections with the early history of chocolate. Sicily has been overrun for centuries by different nations, each leaving behind their cultural influences. The occupying Spaniards long ago brought their chocolate and the method they had learned from the Aztecs of grinding the cacao on a *metate*, a kind of mortar and pestle, and adding spices to it.

Despite the inventions of conching and tempering, the people of Modica remained loyal to the old ways. Northern and central Italy has producers of some of the most refined chocolate in the world (for example, Amedei, see page 70), but Sicily's Antica Dolceria Bonajuto, a business opened in 1880, relishes tradition. Unlike most producers today, they work with pounded cacao that still retains its cocoa butter. It is heated just enough to liquefy the cacao, and caster sugar and flavourings such as vanilla or cinnamon are added. The essence of the technique is that the sugar crystals are not allowed to get warm enough to melt – hence the grainy appearance of sugar and chocolate in the photograph on the facing page. The cooled mixture is then shaped.

Working with cold chocolate creates a very granular chocolate, so it is served in paper cups, as it disintegrates easily, or in bars. It lacks the convenience of a

NAME OF THE BAR *Antica Dolceria Bonajuto Cioccolato di Modica*
COCOA SOLIDS, BLEND OR ORIGIN *None shown*
INGREDIENTS *Sugar, cocoa mass, cinnamon*
WEIGHT OF BAR *100g*
BAR MADE *Modica, Sicily, Italy*
WEBSITE *www.bonajuto.it*
AROMA *Earthy and herbal with notes of tobacco*
TASTE *The texture dominates: the grainy chocolate crumbles in the mouth. A dark chocolate sensation comes through next. The melt is surprisingly light and smooth. The overriding sensation is of sweetness with a spicy finish.*

PROFILE

Floral		Nutty	🦋
Fruity		Spicy	🦋🦋🦋
Winey		Toasty	🦋
Honey	🦋🦋	Smoky	
Creamy	🦋🦋	Earthy	🦋🦋🦋

finely tempered bar, and it certainly lacks the sheen and gloss, but it makes up for all this in sheer personality.

Modica and its chocolate languished in a culinary backwater for decades. However, with the current interest in fine chocolate and the rise of the Slow Food movement and its celebration of local food customs, it is now being rediscovered. It also proves to fans of less processed and 'raw chocolate' such as Pacari (see page 178) that raw chocolate is nothing new. The bars from Claudio Corallo (see page 102) also have that same sense of history.

Artisan du Chocolat

The name of the company may be French but Artisan is keen to stress its Britishness. It is one of the all too few producers in the United Kingdom conching its own chocolate. The company has two shops in fashionable locations in west London. The original store is off Sloane Square, in Chelsea; the other is on Westbourne Grove, in Notting Hill, and with its painted ceiling of a rainforest is just the place to go and enjoy a cocktail made from cacao pulp and soak up the atmosphere.

Irish-born chocolatier Gerard Coleman and his Belgian-born partner Anne Weyns have created a portfolio of chocolates, of which bars are only a part. They are particularly well known for their liquid sea-salted caramels, their iridescent truffle 'pearls' and their slim, flavoured 'O' discs.

The collection of bars is extensive, from single-origin bars to spiced and coffee and tea-flavoured bars. The **Darjeeling Tbar** is deliciously subtle with the slightest hint of moscatel; the **Matcha Green Tbar** is a little more challenging at the outset, given the vivid green colour of the white chocolate. There's even an **Almond Milk** bar for those avoiding dairy, or who love the nutty milk flavour.

ARTISAN du CHOCOLAT*

break the mould

Jamaica
dark chocolate
limited edition

72% Cocoa

ARTISAN du CHOCOLAT
LONDON

TBAR®

FUSION BAR

Darjeeling
dark chocolate
72% Cocoa

Mole Poblano
dark chocolate
70% Cocoa

NAME OF THE BAR *Jamaica Dark Chocolate Limited Edition 72%*
COCOA SOLIDS, BLEND OR ORIGIN *72%, Jamaica*
INGREDIENTS *Cocoa beans, cane sugar, cocoa butter, soya lecithin*
WEIGHT OF BAR *45g*
BAR MADE *Ashford. Kent, UK*
WEBSITE *www.artisanduchocolat.com*
AROMA *Balsamic, roasted black plums, liquorice*
TASTE *The liquorice on the nose follows through on the palate. A light acidity underlines the soft, creamy melt. The flavour develops into fine-grained tar, finishing with darting notes of English lime marmalade.*

PROFILE

Floral		Nutty	❦
Fruity	❦	Spicy	❦
Winey	❦	Toasty	❦❦
Honey	❦❦	Smoky	❦❦
Creamy	❦❦❦	Earthy	❦❦

The bars are cleverly moulded – slim with a ridged shape that allows room for the tongue to explore the melt. However, given the smart packaging of Artisan's other chocolates and the humorous wordsmithing, the bars seem a little chilly by contrast. The lively notes on the back of the packaging are useful to tasters wanting to explore the vocabulary of chocolate and the range is wide enough to satisfy the adventurous.

Askinosie

Once upon a time, Shawn Askinosie was a criminal defence lawyer. It shows in the way he martials the evidence on his website and in his press pack. Where other bean-to-bar producers have attractive materials, and are heavy on charm, Askinosie selects his evidence and puts the (very convincing) message across briskly. Equally he knows that he has only a matter of seconds to capture the attention of the consumer before the wrapper is opened and the chocolate eaten. So he puts all his energies into stopping the chocolate eater in his or her tracks with a flurry of arresting facts and details.

The apparently artless, handmade design of the pack would seem to go against every rule of marketing in the glossy world of chocolate. Askinosie brings it off brilliantly, and with the information on the pack takes on the most important task of telling consumers more about where the chocolate comes from and who made it. (Visitors to Springfield, Missouri, can make a tour of the factory on Tuesdays at 3pm, or by prior arrangement.)

Along the path to making his own chocolate, Shawn Askinosie toyed with the idea of becoming a cupcake king, but thankfully for chocolate lovers he discovered his true vocation. He produces single-origin bars from beans from San José del Tambo, Ecuador; Soconusco, Mexico; and Davao, Philippines (and the wrapper declares 'in 1600 the Spanish bought the first cacao to grow in Asia in the Philippines. Ours is the first Filipino cocoa bean export in nearly 25 years.').

For lovers of white chocolate, it is worth knowing that he says he is 'the only small-batch chocolate maker to make white chocolate in North America from

NAME OF THE BAR *Askinosie San José del Tambo, Ecuador 70%*

COCOA SOLIDS, BLEND OR ORIGIN *70%, Ecuador, Arriba Nacional*

INGREDIENTS *Cocoa beans, organic cane juice, cocoa butter ('made in our factory with del Tambo beans')*

WEIGHT OF BAR *85g*

BAR MADE *Springfield, Missouri, USA*

WEBSITE *www.askinosie.com*

AROMA *Earthy, balsamic, herbal, liquorice*

TASTE *Initially earthy, with a determined tannic grip, dark and firm, softened by a note of honey. Big, savoury and confident.*

PROFILE

Floral		Nutty	🍂
Fruity		Spicy	
Winey		Toasty	🍂🍂
Honey	🍂	Smoky	
Creamy		Earthy	🍂🍂🍂

bean to bar'. I would add that there are not too many in the rest of the world. The fact that he uses goat's milk powder for the white chocolate makes it attractive to people intolerant to dairy; I find it appealing for its lift of acidity, a delicate, almost citrussy note typical of the freshest goat's cheese. A key feature of this ability to make good white chocolate is that Askinosie produces its own cocoa butter from its own beans. It is common practice nowadays among many chocolate producers to add cocoa butter back in, and from a different origin from the cocoa mass. As a bean-to-bar producer, Askinosie can follow the chain of production of his own raw materials.

One distinctive feature of Askinosie chocolate is its emphasis on texture. The string used to tie the packs of chocolate is re-used from the cocoa sacks, and the unbleached, home-compostable wrapper has a grainy-textured surface. Texture is also present in some of the bars – there is a white bar with cocoa nibs (see page 26) and another with roasted, salted pistachios. The 70% **San José del Tambo Nibble Bar** is equally crunchy, as is the **El Rústico** bar with sugar crystals and pieces of vanilla bean.

Bachhalm

Some bars reveal their nationality easily. Bachhalm is one such. The Jugendstil (Art Nouveau) design of the wrappers speaks of Viennese coffee houses of over 100 years ago. The satisfying dark chocolate flavour of the bars demands the creaminess of a Melange, the Viennese frothed milk cappuccino-style drink. It's no surprise that Bachhalm, founded in 1928 in Kirchdorf an der Krems, about 60km (37 miles) south of Linz, is a traditional *konditorei*, an Austrian café/patissier, with an impressive array of sweet treats.

There is an extensive selection of bars, all perfectly if excessively wrapped in protective casing. The flavoured bars are a speciality, including one with candied rose petals pressed on. Some of these bars reveal a certain middle European flavour, most particularly the dark chocolate with white truffle oil and shiitake mushrooms. This is not entirely successful: the oil is integrated but the mushrooms remain desiccated and have a flabby texture in the mouth.

When it comes to flavours in chocolate, it looks as if Austria dominates the alphabet of producers from B (Bachhalm) to Z (Zotter), culminating in Zotter's cheese, walnut and grape bar (see page 226). Personally my choice from Bacchalm is an unadulterated square of **Grand Cru Tanzania** 76% with nibs, or the **Peru 'Alto el Sol'** limited edition 75% (see facing page) both fine origin chocolates that are perfect with a fine origin coffee with a shot of milk.

NAME OF THE BAR *Bachhalm 1928 Pure Selection Handmade Grand Cru Plantation Chocolate*

COCOA SOLIDS, BLEND OR ORIGIN *75%, Peru 'Alto el Sol'*

INGREDIENTS *Cacao mass, sugar, cacao butter, emulsifier: soya lecithin, natural vanilla*

WEIGHT OF BAR *75g*

BAR MADE *Kirchdorf an der Krems, Austria*

WEBSITE *www.bachhalm.at*

AROMA *Warmly chocolatey, mocha, creamy*

TASTE *Begins with a bright, fruity acidity, then notes of roasted coffee and nuts come booming in; the finish is once more bright with a refreshing lift of orangey acidity. Mildly fudgy texture.*

PROFILE

Floral		Nutty	🌶
Fruity	🌶🌶	Spicy	
Winey	🌶	Toasty	🌶🌶
Honey	🌶🌶	Smoky	🌶
Creamy		Earthy	

Bernachon

There are chocolate shops the world over that are painted and decorated to look like French chocolatiers. Bernachon is that rarity, the authentic version. At their shop and tea room in Lyon, the centre of France's culinary universe, the Bernachon family make no compromises. Now in their third generation, they continue to select their beans and roast and conch them on the premises. Most chocolatiers are content to source the best couverture – or finished chocolate – for their purpose from another supplier. Not the Bernachons.

The Bernachons are passionate guardians of fine chocolate. Jean-Jacques, son of the first generation Maurice, is quoted as saying: 'True chocolate can only be made with cocoa butter. All our chocolates wholly respect this tradition.' It is no wonder that the Bernachons were an inspiration to Robert Steinberg, co-founder of Scharffen Berger (see page 200), Richard Donnelly (see page 192) and Alan McClure of Patric (see page 180).

Given the Bernachons' evident success with the citizens of Lyon during the last 50 years, the obvious question is why they have not expanded into other shops. The answer is that quality demands a narrow focus. For a visitor to their one shop, there is no immediate sign that Bernachon is different from any other chocolatier. The proof comes from the bite of the first chocolate bought at the counter.

If there is room in your shopping bag, there is a riot of bars to take away – more than 30 in all. Dark and milk, plain and flavoured, with cocoa nibs, nuts, nougat, orange, cinnamon, coffee, and plenty more. **Coffee with walnuts** (60%) is a

NAME OF THE BAR *Bernachon Amer 70%*
COCOA SOLIDS, BLEND OR ORIGIN *70%*
INGREDIENTS *Not shown*
WEIGHT OF BAR *150g*
BAR MADE *Lyon, France*
WEBSITE *www.bernachon.com*
AROMA *Pure chocolate, with dark elements of tobacco*
TASTE *Mild and chocolatey, smooth and rounded, with a very long finish and a surprisingly refreshing citrus lift. A classic blend.*

PROFILE

Floral		Nutty	𝄞
Fruity	𝄞𝄞𝄞	Spicy	
Winey	𝄞	Toasty	𝄞𝄞𝄞
Honey	𝄞𝄞𝄞	Smoky	𝄞𝄞
Creamy	𝄞	Earthy	𝄞𝄞𝄞

fine blend of mild dark chocolate, strong coffee and sweet nuts. Their precise understanding of their chocolate means that the balance of flavours in their pralines and blends is equally accurate.

Bernard Castelain

The town of Châteauneuf-du-Pape in the southern Rhône Valley is home to one of France's most popular red wines. It is famous for having vineyards full of large flat stones, or *galets*, which reflect their heat back up to the bunches of grapes on the vine. As he is the local chocolatier, Bernard Castelain (who set up shop in 1994) inevitably has to make chocolate *galets* (almonds coated with dark and white chocolate).

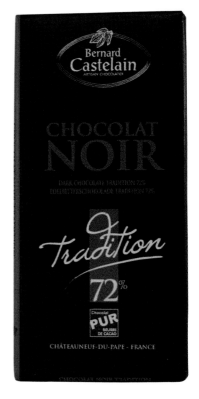

The red wine of Châteauneuf-du-Pape earns its place in the wine textbooks because it is blended from as many as 13 grape varieties. Castelain also makes blends, from 37% cocoa solids to 99%, the origins ranging from South America to Africa, although by no means as many as 13.

Of the bars in the Castelain range, the 85% is surprisingly successful, given my personal reservations about dark chocolate with such a high percentage of cocoa solids. It has an appealing aroma of red berry fruits, suggesting a sweeter, lower cocoa solids bar, yet is remarkably powerful and full of flavour given that so many of these bars can be bitter and one-dimensional.

Castelain also makes single-origin bars; the range currently includes bars from Ecuador, Santo Domingo (in the Dominican Republic), Tanzania and South America. The latter, called **Macaïbo**, is a welcome contrast to the punchiness of so many new bars; the flavour is the essence of chocolate, in a gentle and mild expression. This is definitely a bar to enjoy by itself, as it would be swamped by coffee, or after the strong flavours of a spicy meal.

NAME OF THE BAR *Bernard Castelain Chocolat Noir Tradition 72%*
COCOA SOLIDS, BLEND OR ORIGIN *72% 'made with the Grand Crus of cacao from South America and Africa'*
INGREDIENTS *Cocoa mass, sugar, cocoa butter, Bourbon vanilla*
WEIGHT OF BAR *100g*
BAR MADE *Châteauneuf-du-Pape, Vaucluse, France*
WEBSITE *www.chocolat-castelain.com*
AROMA *Dark dense and savoury with tobacco notes*
TASTE *Starts slowly and develops gradually into a delicately nutty, smoky profile. Altogether subtle and understated, the essence of a satisfying dark blend.*

PROFILE

Floral		Nutty	🌿
Fruity		Spicy	
Winey		Toasty	🌿
Honey	🌿	Smoky	🌿🌿
Creamy		Earthy	🌿🌿

Beschle

There is something supremely confident about Dominic and Pascal Beschle's bars with their lightly corrugated card wrapper, the family crest and cocoa pod engraving, and their gold foil inner. They are elegant, too – just the thing for a Swiss banker to produce from a discreet leather portfolio.

The family, now in its fourth generation, has had over a century in Basel to polish the recipes. Beschle started as a *confiserie* in 1898 and it was only when Dominic Beschle took over in 2006 that chocolate production was set up as a separate business in order to expand and build exports. Dominic works with his brother Paul, the Maître Choco-latier. Despite the classical glamour of the packaging Beschle is keen to stress that it offers 'innovative and unusual creations with a touch of eccentricity, as well as chocolate craftsmanship'. Those who find chocolate spreads too rich should try Beschle's spread with nibs; though not exactly eccentric, the nibs do add texture and character.

Beschle's bars soothe and seduce with classic flavours rather than shock with wild ones. The milk bar, **Grand Cru au Lait** 38%, has the typical Swiss milki-ness, full of cream, caramel, honey and nougat, with a tart lift on the finish. The white chocolate bar, **Ivoire aux Amandes & Myrtilles**, is bursting dramati-cally with dark blueberries and almonds. Both in colour contrast – the dark berries protruding slightly against the smoothness of the immaculate ivory chocolate – and in taste, it is a tempting creation, although it is sweet. The Quizás label is the Venezuelan single-origin range, introduced in 2007. These bars come wrapped in gold foil and encased in elegant ribbed card folders, which include plenty of information on the inside. The Beschles are obviously respectful of the origins and present the bars with care.

NAME OF THE BAR *Beschle Quizás No 1 Premier Cru Criollo*
COCOA SOLIDS, BLEND OR ORIGIN *74%, Criollo Porcelana Zulia Venezuela,*
'48 hour conch by the traditional method'
INGREDIENTS *Cocoa mass, cocoa butter, cane sugar, 'without lecithin'*
WEIGHT OF BAR *50g*
BAR MADE *Basel, Switzerland*
WEBSITE *www.beschlechocolatier.com*
AROMA *Bold and deep, floral, herbal, liquorice*
TASTE *A gentle build to a powerful mouthful, well-balanced. Flavours of roasted mocha and nuts with caramel. A smooth, supple melt.*

PROFILE

Floral		Nutty	❧❧❧
Fruity	❧❧	Spicy	❧
Winey	❧	Toasty	❧❧
Honey	❧❧❧	Smoky	
Creamy	❧❧❧	Earthy	❧

Bianco & Nero

Most visitors to Mendoza in Argentina come for the wine; some are in transit west to or across the Andes to Chile, or south to Patagonia. A few arrive for the polo. None expect to come to this sunny, dusty, bustling city for chocolate. I certainly did not. So I was delighted when, while visiting the Trapiche winery, I came across samples of Roberto Aguero's chocolate left over from a tasting. The chief winemaker, Daniel Pi, is an enthusiast for Roberto's work, and likes to match the chocolate with his wine.

In general, I am not keen on matching dry red wines (or dry whites, for that matter) with dark chocolate. However, Argentina has made a speciality of the grape variety Malbec, which produces ripe, occasionally syrupy reds, high in alcohol. These have enough supple fruitiness to pair with some types of

NAME OF THE BAR *Bianco & Nero Grand Cru Esmeraldas 70% Cacao Ecuador*
COCOA SOLIDS, BLEND OR ORIGIN *70%, Esmeraldas, Ecuador*
INGREDIENTS *Not shown*
WEIGHT OF BAR *60g*
BAR MADE *Mendoza, Argentina*
WEBSITE *www.bianco-nero.com.ar*
AROMA *Creamy, nutty, mildly chocolatey*
TASTE *More deeply chocolatey than the aromas would suggest, developing a roasted mocha profile with bright notes of tropical fruits. Long finish with grain of tannin.*

PROFILE

Floral		Nutty	🌶
Fruity	🌶🌶🌶	Spicy	
Winey	🌶🌶	Toasty	🌶
Honey	🌶🌶🌶	Smoky	
Creamy	🌶🌶🌶	Earthy	🌶🌶

chocolate. On my second visit to the winery I made a point of meeting Roberto Aguero there and tasting through his range of chocolates with him in the room where the wine tastings are held.

Like many of today's chocolate artisans, Aguero had a previous career – he was a lawyer in Buenos Aires. While recuperating from an illness, he discovered the pleasure of cooking for his family. Then, in southern Argentina he met an 82-year-old woman who had learnt the art of chocolate-making from a Swiss. The two exchanged recipes, and his new career had begun. It is no surprise that this encounter happened in the south; the lakeside city of Bariloche is renowned for its chocolate. This is partly because of the amenable cool climate, but mainly because of the long tradition of German and Swiss settlers, who brought their food culture and experience with them.

At Bianco & Nero, Aguero makes chocolate from South American origins only – his main supplier of couverture is Fenix in Buenos Aires. Almost two decades after his sudden career break, the world of chocolate has overtaken him. In addition to his origin bars, he makes a whole range of truffles, bonbons, patisserie and more which he sells from his shops in Mendoza City.

Blanxart

Blanxart could only be Catalan. First, the 'x' (pronounced 'sh') is a bit of a giveaway. Second, the brand logo speaks of Catalonia's bold, intelligent approach to design. The original image was found in a local museum's archives. Its antique appearance cleverly echoes Spain's history in the world of chocolate. Third, many of the ingredients used by Blanxart are identifiably Spanish, if not exactly Catalan: Marcona almonds, hazelnuts from Reus and *piñones* (pine kernels) from Castile. The range includes 'chocolate de taza' (drinking chocolate), a reminder that Spain is a country that savours its drinking chocolate rich and thick. No morning in the market, or late night at a traditional *feria*, is complete without the opportunity to dip deep-fried fresh *churros* into the unctuous liquid.

NAME OF THE BAR *Blanxart Chocolate Ecológico Negro 72%*

COCOA SOLIDS, BLEND OR ORIGIN *72%, organic*

INGREDIENTS *Cocoa, raw cane sugar, cocoa butter, emulsifier (lecithin), natural vanilla flavour*

WEIGHT OF BAR *100g*

BAR MADE *Barcelona, Spain*

WEBSITE *www.blanxart.com*

AROMA *Dark, earthy, deeply chocolatey*

TASTE *Starts very dark with molasses and treacle, and a strong flavour from the raw cane sugar. A fudgy melt, resulting in a resoundingly rib-sticking bar.*

PROFILE

Floral		Nutty	✿✿✿
Fruity		Spicy	
Winey		Toasty	✿✿
Honey	✿✿✿	Smoky	✿
Creamy	✿	Earthy	✿✿

Blanxart was founded in 1954, when a master chocolatier set up a business in Barcelona with four partners. Today, Blanxart sources beans from Ghana and the Dominican Republic and roasts and conches them in the factory. The range is extensive, offering every kind of filled chocolate.

The bars offer a full range of flavours, some traditional, some more surprising, including the exotic range of **Kenyan Peanuts, Ethiopian Coffee, Ceylon Cinnamon** and **Madras Curry**, the latter in a white chocolate bar.

Cacao Sampaka

Cacao Sampaka started in Barcelona in 2000 and is part of the city's vibrant chocolate revolution, which also includes the highly regarded chocolatier Oriol Balaguer, Blanxart (see page 90) and the inventive Enric Rovira (see page 118). Cacao Sampaka's shops, now in a number of cities in Spain, Portugal, Tokyo and elsewhere, express the very essence of Spanish style. They are temples to chocolate, with a post-modern feel. Partly it is the effect of the cafés, where customers can stop for a thick hot chocolate, or something stronger. The wine list is an intelligent selection of wines, cavas and liqueurs chosen to match the chocolate. There is always a buzz about the shops, together with the kind of refinement that is missing from the average coffee chain store.

The layout of the shops is bright, lacking some of the brown gloom that pervades shops filled with brown chocolates and staff in brown uniform.

Packaging is discreet and modern. The chocolates themselves are tempting – or at least most of them are. For among the almond rochers, the chocolate-coated cocoa nibs, the fruit-flavoured chocolates, there is the 'gastronomic innovations' box. This is the box to buy for someone who likes an adventure – but I find anchovy, for instance, is a flavour that is worth trying only once. It is more fun to stay with 'single bean origins' or 'dried fruit and nuts'.

Compared with the glamour and drama of the rest of the shop, the bars look less exciting. They are hermetically sealed, which protects them but lacks charm. Each pack contains two slim, nicely snappy 50g bars. There are plain bars in white, milk, bitter and dark; origin bars, including Xoconusco from Mexico; and flavoured bars, grouped into 'families', including crunchy, innovations and sugar-free.

NAME OF THE BAR *Cacao Sampaka Chocolate Negro 70%*
COCOA SOLIDS, BLEND OR ORIGIN *70%*
INGREDIENTS *Cocoa mass, sugar, cocoa butter, emulsifier soy lecithin, natural vanilla flavouring*
WEIGHT OF BAR *100g (2 x 50g)*
BAR MADE *Barcelona, Spain*
WEBSITE *www.cacaosampaka.com*
AROMA *Coffee, liquorice, smoke and earth*
TASTE *A mild blend, with notes of green apple, mint and aniseed. The melt is very smooth – almost cool and minty. A tannic bite comes in just at the end to add definition.*

PROFILE

Floral	🍫	Nutty	🍫
Fruity	🍫🍫	Spicy	
Winey	🍫	Toasty	🍫
Honey	🍫🍫	Smoky	🍫
Creamy	🍫🍫🍫	Earthy	🍫🍫

Above: Step inside: as the signs on the pillars indicate, the Sampaka shops are full of temptations.

Chococo

I must confess I was somewhat doubtful when I first walked into Chococo's colourful, welcoming shop in a back street in Swanage, one of England's favourite seaside towns along the South Coast. Surely, given all the fish and chip and surf gear shops, open only for the summer season, Chococo would only sell the cheapest confectionery to the bucket and spade brigade on the beach? How wrong I was!

Andy Burnet is a local man, and knows the town as well as anyone. His wife, Claire, is determined to make fine chocolate available to all their customers, and at the same time to introduce them to chocolate-making. That's why the factory has a window onto the street, to draw in customers, and to show that there is nothing to hide. In this respect the Burnets perform an important service because they are so clearly on view, rather than hiding away in a discreet, elegant upmarket store. Like other producers, Chococo has to get out there and fight the fine chocolate war.

The Burnets represent a new generation in chocolate, who are coming to it as a second career. They have swapped successful jobs in marketing and finance for long hours in chocolate, with the occasional chance to enjoy the countryside with their family. Their skills in marketing and finance are definitely a help: their chocolates and bars looked professional and distinctive from the start, in 2002, and they have won a number of awards.

Bars are not Chococo's main activity, but they are given the same lively treatment as the filled chocolates and truffles. The square 125g bars are drizzled with decorative flavours: dark and milk bars infused with orange oil and scattered with candied orange peel; white chocolate infused with yogurt and

NAME OF THE BAR *Dark on Dark Bar*

COCOA SOLIDS, BLEND OR ORIGIN *73%, Venezuela*

INGREDIENTS *Cocoa mass, sugar, cocoa butter, soya lecithin, natural vanilla, roasted cocoa nibs, raisins, gum Arabic, coffee*

WEIGHT OF BAR *125g*

BAR MADE *Swanage, Dorset, England*

WEBSITE *www.chococo.co.uk*

AROMA *Lifted notes of coconut and cream, with a promise of dark chocolate*

TASTE *A dense, dark chocolate experience, relieved by the occasional note of coffee, or crunch of nib. Long and persistent, with the faintest bite of tannin at the very end.*

PROFILE

Floral		Nutty	❦❦
Fruity	❦❦	Spicy	❦
Winey		Toasty	❦
Honey		Smoky	❦❦❦
Creamy	❦❦	Earthy	❦❦

sprinkled with crushed dried raspberries; and dark and milk bars studded with nuts. Their couverture suppliers include the Venezuelan El Rey (see page 116) who produce the Icoa white chocolate they use. Made from a relatively high amount (34%) of 'non-deodorised' cocoa butter, it's a white chocolate that tastes of so much more than sugar and milk powder.

Chocolat Bonnat

For many years, French families driving south to the mountains to ski have acquired the habit of stopping off at the Bonnat shop in Voiron to take some treats with them for those après-ski moments. The Bonnat bars were among the first bars that I came to recognise as a child, as they were among my father's favourites. This availability in England is an indicator of Bonnat's established export success. I was enchanted by the packaging, although I did not like the chocolate then, thinking it too bitter.

At the time I did not realise that I was nibbling a piece of chocolate history, for the Bonnats believe that they are the oldest family firm in the world still producing handmade chocolates starting from the cacao bean.(Click on the 'Glossary' button on the website; under the definition of 'Winnower' there is a brief recording of their elderly winnowing machine, bringing the rough and tumble journey of the cacao bean vividly to life.)

NAME OF THE BAR *Chocolat Bonnat Chuao Village 'Venezuela' 75%*
COCOA SOLIDS, BLEND OR ORIGIN *75%, Chuao Village, Venezuela*
INGREDIENTS *Cocoa, cocoa butter, sugar*
WEIGHT OF BAR *100g*
BAR MADE *Voiron, Isère, France*
WEBSITE *www.bonnat-chocolatier.com*
AROMA *Red fruit, red wine, citrus, dark chocolate*
TASTE *A brisk beginning, with tight, firm acidity, gives way to a silky chocolate character. Broad, rich mid-palate. Tarry, tannic finish, full of flavour.*

PROFILE

Floral		Nutty	✿✿
Fruity	✿	Spicy	
Winey	✿✿	Toasty	✿✿
Honey	✿✿✿	Smoky	✿
Creamy		Earthy	✿✿✿

Bonnat bars cover the classic origins with their 'Grands Crus' range, including **Apotequil**, a typically pale-coloured Porcelana cacao from Peru which has citrus and plum fruit with prunes on the finish, and **Marfil de Blanco**, a Porcelana from Mexico, a very delicate chocolate with mint highlights. The **Cacao Real del Xoconuzco** from Mexico (75%) has a vivid profile of roasted nuts and toast.

The ingredients of these Cru bars are simply cacao, cocoa butter and sugar, without an emulsifier or vanilla. This helps an interested taster to learn about the different flavours of the origins. Their maker, Stéphane Bonnat, in his pristine white coat, has the contented air of a boyish dentist who is pleased to find that the world is suddenly discovering what he already knows.

It is a pity that the bars lack the sensible protective wrapping used by newer producers, and to taste they often have a grainy character. This is surprising, given the seriousness of the business and its long experience with cacao. Nevertheless, the existence of an independent family identity can only be applauded when so much of the chocolate world is dominated by takeovers and global brands.

Chocolate Santander

Coffee and chocolate, Colombia produces them both. In the Chocolate Santander bars, especially the **Semi-dark** 53%, the two seem to mingle. There is the apparent milkiness of a cappuccino with a single coffee shot, finishing with the tannic bite of a high roast coffee – and it is sweet, with a dash of red fruit, suggesting one of the flavouring syrups. While some bars are an intellectual challenge, these are chocolate bars that are meant to be fun to eat, as befits a nation that enjoys both chocolate and chocolate confectionery.

Chocolate Santander is the fine chocolate brand of Compañia Nacional de Chocolates, set up in 1920, and currently the only single origin producer in Colombia. The brand takes its name from the region of production, Santander in eastern Colombia, which lies across the mountains from the Sur del Lago region of Venezuela and its famed cacaos. Santander has both Trinitario and Criollo cacaos, and there are undoubted genetic similarities with the Venezuelan cacaos.

The business is strong on social responsibility, and the support it gives to its workers and their dependants. The tradition of cacao-growing dates back two centuries in the Santander region and nowadays it supports some 12,000 families.

The range of chocolate includes, appropriately enough, chocolate-coated coffee beans and a 70% bar with 'Coffee Bits' or crushed coffee. The plain bars range from 36% to 75% – the latter is a vintage bar, giving an expression of the year, without vanilla to obscure the flavour. Santander is one of the few chocolate producers to declare a vintage.

NAME OF THE BAR *Chocolate Santander Colombian Single Origin Dark Chocolate 70%*
COCOA SOLIDS, BLEND OR ORIGIN *70%, Santander department, Colombia*
INGREDIENTS *Cocoa mass, cocoa powder, cocoa butter, emulsifier (soy lecithin), natural vanilla*
WEIGHT OF BAR *70g*
BAR MADE *Rionegro, Santander, Colombia*
WEBSITE *www.chocolatesantander.com*
AROMA *Brightly lifted aromas of vanilla, mint and dark chocolate*
TASTE *Starts fudgy and a little hollow; finally the chocolate flavour comes through, with a creamy profile of hazelnuts, dark toast, a note of tobacco and roasted coffee, and a clean, mildly grainy finish.*

PROFILE

Floral		Nutty	❦❦
Fruity		Spicy	❦
Winey		Toasty	❦❦
Honey	❦❦	Smoky	❦❦
Creamy	❦❦	Earthy	❦

Above: Evenly dried beans are crucial for flavour development. Depending on the sun, the process takes between five and eight days. This is Chocolate Santander's experimental farm.

Choxi

CHOXI was one of the first widely available chocolates to tune in to the trend of 'chocolate as health food', boasting that it is 'naturally rich in antioxidants'. It is processed at lower temperatures than most other chocolate, thereby it is said retaining more of the cocoa bean's beneficial antioxidants. The amount of antioxidants depends on the amount of cocoa solids. The bars are marked to make the 'daily dose' easier to follow; thus the dark bar is divided into 5g squares and the milk into 12.5g squares.

Cocoa beans are rich in a group of antioxidants called flavanols, which seem to be particularly effective at neutralising potentially harmful free radicals. The back of the pack explains: 'By preserving the goodness of cocoa, CHOXI+ dark chocolate contains 2.2% cocoa flavanols, twice as much as a standard dark chocolate. A small piece of CHOXI+ each day is a positive indulgence anyone can enjoy.' This is a rare chocolate bar that encourages people to eat only a small amount.

CHOXI uses Acticoa chocolate, developed by chocolate giant Barry Callebaut, which claims to preserve the flavanols in cacao at each stage of production. The website *www.acticoa.com* explains the broad outlines of how the cacao bean promotes health, and also has a comparative chart of flavanol values. It claims that a pear and a bunch of red grapes has the same amount of antioxidants as 8.7g of Acticoa dark chocolate.

NAME OF THE BAR *CHOXI Dark Chocolate 70%*
COCOA SOLIDS, BLEND OR ORIGIN *70%*
INGREDIENTS *Cocoa mass, sugar, fat-reduced cocoa powder, anhydrous milk fat, emulsifier (soya lecithin), natural vanilla*
WEIGHT OF BAR *70g*
BAR MADE *London, England*
WEBSITE *www.choxiplus.com*
AROMA *A honeyed, creamy profile, with light notes of roasted almonds*
TASTE *The chocolate starts smooth and fudgey, then the flavour disappears. Finally, it comes surging back with dry leather and green tannin, and over-roasted coffee beans.*

PROFILE

Floral		Nutty	🌶
Fruity	🌶	Spicy	🌶🌶
Winey		Toasty	🌶🌶🌶
Honey	🌶	Smoky	🌶🌶
Creamy		Earthy	🌶🌶🌶

Functional foods have a good deal of appeal in a time-poor, high-stress society. Making a chocolate that has health benefits is obviously a clever piece of marketing. However, the most important thing is that the bar should be good to eat. In this respect the **Dark Chocolate with Stem Ginger** is more appealing than the 70% bar reviewed above, as its crystalline crunchiness masks the bitter roast. Also in the range are **Milk**, **Milk with Sweet Orange** and **Dark Chocolate with Oriental Mint**. For chocolate lovers, this remains a work in progress.

Claudio Corallo

Claudio Corallo is one of the heroic characters of today's chocolate revolution. Not content with sourcing fine beans and building close working relationships with the growers, he lives with his family in the zone of production where he grows the cacao and makes the chocolate. Corallo is Italian, and trained as an agronomist. His original career was in Zaire (now the Democratic Republic of Congo), where he worked with coffee, and eventually he bought two plantations of his own. His long experience of working with the plants and the people, in challenging isolation, stood him in good stead. When he and his family were obliged to leave their home because of civil war, they moved to the similarly isolated islands of São Tomé and Príncipe, tucked in off the west coast of Africa.

Corallo's ex-wife Bettina, daughter of Portugal's ambassador to Zaire, had found excellent quality cacao and coffee on a trip to the islands. This convinced the family to settle on Príncipe and attempt to revive an abandoned industry. The Portuguese had brought cacao to their African island colony in 1823, from Bahia in Brazil. Corallo is working now with a version of Forastero cacao known as Amelonado, from the melon shape of the pods.

Corallo's aim is to reflect the pure character of his cacao. The harvested cacao is taken to the adjoining island of São Tomé for fermenting, drying and sorting. Not for Corallo the polished smoothness of many Italian chocolate makers – his chocolate remains coarsely ground to preserve aromas and flavours. Despite his isolated situation, his chocolate is beginning to get distribution. In addition to the dark bars, including a 100%, there are flavoured bars: one with orange, one with ginger. Look out for the **Ubric** bar, a rugged treat of raisins soaked in wild cherry liqueur.

NAME OF THE BAR *Claudio Corallo Chocolate Soft 70% com nibs de cacau*

COCOA SOLIDS, BLEND OR ORIGIN *70% , Terreiro Velho, Príncipe*

INGREDIENTS *Cacao, sugar, cocoa butter*

WEIGHT OF BAR *100g*

BAR MADE *São Tomé, West Africa*

WEBSITE *www.claudiocorallochocolate.com*

AROMA *Deeply earthy, leafy and balsamic*

TASTE *Brisk and bold, with all the wild energy of cacao that has not been intensely processed. Tannins on the finish are well-managed. The nibs add an appealing texture and dash of bitterness.*

PROFILE

Floral		Nutty	🌱
Fruity		Spicy	
Winey	🌱🌱	Toasty	🌱🌱
Honey		Smoky	🌱
Creamy		Earthy	🌱🌱🌱

CoCouture

Belfast-born Deirdre McCanny originally trained as a chef, but then abandoned the kitchen for a high-powered job in international sales and marketing. She returned from New York in 2008 to set up her own chocolate business, taking the view that the demand for fine chocolate was sufficiently strong. Success came rapidly, for in 2009 she won Gold from the Academy of Chocolate for her **Milk Chocolate with Honeycomb** bar and Bronze for her **Dark Chocolate with Rum and Raisin**.

McCanny's rapid success is not altogether surprising – in addition to her chef skills, she had prepared for the business by taking specialist classes with a Spanish chocolatier. From the outset she was determined to focus on quality: she uses French and Italian couverture from top producers such as Amedei (see page 70). This is where she can show her skill as a chocolatier, taking couvertures which are good already, then blending and tempering them to create something individual. For a new chocolate business blending is also useful, because the fine couvertures are expensive to buy, and subtle blending helps to keep its prices competitive.

Given her previous experience in marketing, it is not surprising that McCanny's bars and chocolates are so desirably packaged. The bars are wrapped in foil paper, with a textured card box in a toning colour. The bars themselves are beautifully finished in moulds decorated with cacao flowers and leaves, and McCanny has taken to giving each bar a signature piece of gold leaf in one corner.

NAME OF THE BAR *CoCouture Blend II 69% dark chocolate*

COCOA SOLIDS, BLEND OR ORIGIN *69%*

INGREDIENTS *Dark chocolate (cocoa solids, sugar, cocoa butter, vanilla, soya lecithin)*

WEIGHT OF BAR *50g*

BAR MADE *Belfast, Northern Ireland*

WEBSITE *www.cocouture.co.uk*

AROMA *Roasted cocoa with citrus and green leaves*

TASTE *Rises through a basis of dark chocolate to tangy citrus notes with molasses. The finish is persistent, with flavours of brown sugar.*

PROFILE

Floral	❦❦	Nutty	❦
Fruity	❦❦❦	Spicy	
Winey	❦	Toasty	
Honey	❦	Smoky	❦
Creamy	❦	Earthy	❦

At times she feels the isolation in Belfast – she says she lacks the companion-ship of a local community of chocolatiers with whom to taste and share information and experience. Despite this she is making a convincing start, keeping her range of bars and truffles small and focusing on selling these in the United Kingdom and United States, the consumers she knows best.

Dagoba

Frederick Schilling started Dagoba, an organic brand with an emphasis on sustainability, in 2001. At that time Dagoba filled a real gap in the US fine chocolate market for organic chocolate. The business grew rapidly, demanding the assistance of Frederick's family and friends. That partly explains, he says, why Dagoba was sold to The Hershey Company in 2006, in a move that might crudely be seen as the little good guy selling out to big bad business. Craig Sams of Green and Black's (see page 128), and John Scharffenberger (see page 200) both faced similar criticism.

Schilling moved on, pursuing his interests in sustainable projects, and taking on another chocolate project, AMMA (see page 72). In the meantime, the Dagoba brand retains its organic identity alongside a range of ethical initiatives in the cacao-growing countries. Seed the Day is a long-term reforestation project in Costa Rica that engages consumers – practically conceived and simply explained on the website.

Dagoba's bars have always been distinctive, not just for the Dagoba name on each finger of the bar, but also for their mildly rustic finish. The balance of the

NAME OF THE BAR *Dagoba Organic Chocolate New Moon 74%*
COCOA SOLIDS, BLEND OR ORIGIN *74%, organic*
INGREDIENTS *Organic dark chocolate (organic cacao beans, organic cane sugar, organic cacao butter, non-GMO soy lecithin, organic milk (less than 0.1%)*
WEIGHT OF BAR *56g*
BAR MADE *Ashland, Oregon, USA*
WEBSITE *www.dagobachocolate.com*
AROMA *Floral and darkly chocolatey with prunes, raisins and nuts*
TASTE *Dark, molasses profile, grainy texture which lacks depth.*

PROFILE

Floral		Nutty	🌟
Fruity		Spicy	🌟
Winey	🌟	Toasty	🌟🌟
Honey	🌟	Smoky	
Creamy	🌟🌟	Earthy	🌟

chocolate has been uneven, but as with all organic brands their consumers defend them loyally. There are more than 15 different bars at the time of writing: the plain bars extend from 87% to 37% cocoa solids and there are single origin bars, as well as 'exotic' flavoured ones. The **Superfruit** (74%) bar includes acai and goji berries; **Lemon Ginger** (68%) has lemon essence and crystallised ginger; **Chai** has chai tea spices in a 37% milk bar; my least favourite is the **Lavender Blueberry** bar – I recognise that lavender has calming properties if inhaled, but as far as I'm concerned, it's just not for eating. Count me out on that one.

Finally, what about the company name, which fans of Star Wars will recognise as being similar to that of the planet Dagobah? Both words stem from a corruption of the Sanskrit word for a stupa or reliquary mound.

De Bondt

De Bondt is not a producer for the indecisive. Think of almost any chocolate bar you would like to try, and Paul de Bondt and Cecilia Iacobelli will have made it already. Choosing just one from their range is an impossibility. Paul is Dutch, and the quality of his chocolate and sensitive use of flavourings reveal his years of practice as a pastry chef. Cecilia is a designer from Tuscany – her packaging is restrained and thoughtful, ensuring strong flavours do not contaminate other chocolates nearby.

Their portfolio covers every kind of chocolate. Focusing on the bars, it's enough to say that their classic range of 100g bars consists of a remarkable collection of: white, milk (31%, 33%, 38%, 45%), dark (60%, 66%, 70% [see profile facing page], 71%, 80%, 90%, 100%), plus 'no sugar' bars made with the sugar substitute maltitol. There are distinct flavour profiles between the bars, even between 68% and 71%, so this is one company where it is important to sample the range to find your favourite.

Then there are the aromatic bars, in nine categories, ranging from 'Sensual' to 'Crystals'– there are 24 flavours altogether. In addition, there are no less than four bars flavoured with different strengths and types of chilli. The milk bar (45%) **Oro e Caramello** (with gold and caramel) on the facing page is a sheer indulgence of caramel crunchiness topped with gold leaf. If there is a flavour worth trying, then Paul de Bondt has thought about it.

NAME OF THE BAR *De Bondt Cioccolato Fondente 70%*

COCOA SOLIDS, BLEND OR ORIGIN *70%, 'Forastero and Trinitario from various origins'*

INGREDIENTS *Cocoa mass, sugar, emulsifier (soya lecithin)*

WEIGHT OF BAR *100g*

BAR MADE *Visignano, Pisa, Tuscany, Italy*

WEBSITE *www.debondt.it*

AROMA *Creamy and chocolatey with red plums*

TASTE *Full-bodied and solidly chocolatey. It carries its 70% lightly. Undertones of red plums in vanilla cream, rich mid-palate and final grip of tannin.*

PROFILE

Floral		Nutty	🍫
Fruity	🍫🍫	Spicy	🍫
Winey		Toasty	🍫🍫🍫
Honey	🍫	Smoky	🍫🍫🍫
Creamy	🍫🍫	Earthy	🍫🍫

Demarquette

From management consultant to chocolatier: it is an uncommon move, but it is one that Marc Demarquette has made with ease. What undoubtedly helped him was his French heritage. His change in career came suddenly, after an accident, which inevitably caused him to reassess his priorities in life. Born in the United Kingdom to a French father and a Chinese mother, he went to Paris to train in patisserie at the famous cookery school run by the late Gaston LeNôtre. While he had to learn the skills of chocolate, his management experience has surely helped his business planning. Demarquette set up shop on London's Fulham Road in 2005.

His approach to chocolate reflects his varied background: a mix of British ingredients, Chinese spices and French refinement. His preferred couverture is the French Valrhona (see page 216). Among his British ingredients for his chocolates is tea, but this is from an unusual source, the United Kingdom's first tea plantation at the Tregothnan Estate in Cornwall.

When it comes to chocolate bars, Demarquette makes a range of house blends to cater for customer demand. While Valrhona remains a favoured couverture, he is using other suppliers in order to be able to increase his range of origin chocolates. In all he has 15 origin bars, at varying levels of cocoa solids from 64% to 80%, offering a wide choice of flavours from around the world.

Chocolatiers today are expected not only to make chocolates and sell them, they have to be entertainers, too. They need to demonstrate their skills in front of an audience, and

NAME OF THE BAR *Demarquette Rich Blend 76%*
COCOA SOLIDS, BLEND OR ORIGIN *76%*
INGREDIENTS *Cocoa mass, cocoa butter, cane sugar, vanilla, soya lecithin*
WEIGHT OF BAR *80g*
BAR MADE *London, England*
WEBSITE *www.demarquette.com*
AROMA *Elegantly dark*
TASTE *The flavours develop in parallel, with freshness and a dense chocolate character. Well balanced with a slightly grainy grip on the finish.*

PROFILE

Floral	🌱	Nutty	🌱
Fruity		Spicy	
Winey	🌱🌱	Toasty	🌱🌱
Honey	🌱	Smoky	🌱🌱
Creamy	🌱	Earthy	🌱

keep children entertained at parties, and adults at every kind of fund-raising and team-building activity. That is where Marc Demarquette's previous career comes in so handy. When there is a team-building or corporate activity for city types and management folk, then he is the man with the chocolates to charm.

Divine

There is more to Divine than making and selling chocolate. Since the first bar launched in 1998, it has taught a whole generation of UK consumers about where chocolate comes from, and what the term Fairtrade means. Divine has made 'doing good' both fun and delicious. It has also managed to make a complex ownership structure work. The Day Chocolate Company, as it was first called, was a joint project between the forward-looking Kuapa Kokoo co-operative in Ghana, the UK non-governmental organisation Twin Trading, and the ethical cosmetics company, the Body Shop, with the help of Christian Aid and the Comic Relief charity. Over time the balance of ownership has changed, with the co-operative increasing its share. The name of the company has changed too, to match the name of its chocolate brand, Divine.

Divine's success has been in selling itself as a mainstream chocolate bar with a heart of gold. Slowly the rest of the chocolate world is coming to meet its ethical standards, with both Cadbury and Nestlé introducing Fairtrade options to some of their well-known brands. Artisan producers with close ties to their growers may indeed do more for their communities than Fairtrade, but Divine's contribution has been to get chocolate lovers, and especially the young, to think twice about what they eat. The website is a case in point, with its link for resources for teachers. Sign up to the Pa Pa Paa scheme, and classes can watch live webcasts from a school in Ghana.

Divine is also beginning to expand its range, with seasonal products such as Easter eggs, as well as flavoured bars. Do all the flavours succeed? No, but no one's perfect. Do they want to be treated as a special case, because they are Fairtrade? Definitely not. Unwrap the 100g bar and read the inside of the wrapper. There they explain why every bar makes a difference.

NAME OF THE BAR *Divine 70% Dark Chocolate*

COCOA SOLIDS, BLEND OR ORIGIN *70%, Ghana*

INGREDIENTS *Fairtrade cocoa mass, Fairtrade sugar, Fairtrade cocoa butter, soya lecithin (non GM), Fairtrade vanilla*

WEIGHT OF BAR *100g*

BAR MADE *Germany*

WEBSITE *www.divinechocolate.com*

AROMA *Earthy, vanilla, caramel*

TASTE *Mild, with a round, soft, rich palate, gentle tannins and a fairly short finish.*

PROFILE

Floral	Nutty ✿
Fruity	Spicy
Winey	Toasty ✿
Honey ✿	Smoky ✿
Creamy ✿	Earthy ✿

Above: The human face of cacao production in Ghana, the world's second largest producer.

Domori

Very occasionally I encounter a chocolate bar that jumps out of its wrapping and grabs me by the throat. Domori does just that, but in the nicest, most elegant Italian fashion, of course. The effect is all the more surprising because the Domori packaging is such a subtle sell. The box suggests Armani velvet rather than Lamborghini punch. Inside, the wrapper to the bar is equally discreet. It also provokes a small frisson of disappointment, with the realisation that the bar is just a bit smaller than the glamorous box suggests. Rip open the wrapping, though, and any disappointment is blown away by the powerful, sumptuous aromas.

What is impressive about Domori is that the quality is so consistent. While Il Blend (reviewed here) scores high points all round, for sheer eating pleasure as well as technical quality, this is a rare producer that manages to express the differences between the beans and the different origins so well. Domori's tasting notes are also very good for someone wanting to learn how to extend their tasting vocabulary. **Puertofino** (70%) is described on the back as 'notes of caramel, tobacco, walnuts, papaya, brushwood, mushrooms and dates'. Exactly! **Puertomar** (75%) has 'cream, spices, almonds and cherry jam with excellent smoothness and sweetness'. I agree, though they have missed the echo of bitterness from the 75% cacao.

There is the occasional bar that will divide consumers. For me this is **Blanco-liquirizia**, a white chocolate made from Peruvian Apurimac cocoa butter with Calabrian liquorice. It is an ambitious attempt and shows that Domori is prepared to lead fashion, not just to follow it, but it is not a flavour that I wish to taste again.

NAME OF THE BAR *Domori Il Blend Fine Cacao*
COCOA SOLIDS, BLEND OR ORIGIN *70%, 'a harmony among six cru, where the protagonist is cacao criollo'*
INGREDIENTS *Cocoa mass, cane sugar*
WEIGHT OF BAR *50g*
BAR MADE *Turin, Italy*
WEBSITE *www.domori.com*

AROMA *Powerful, bursting with individuality, showing red fruits, blueberries and flower blossoms*
TASTE *Begins with the impression of crunchy sour cherries in creamy mascarpone with plenty of lime acidity. The finish is all Florentine leather and tobacco with a dash of espresso at the end.*

PROFILE

Floral	🍀	Nutty	
Fruity	🍀🍀🍀	Spicy	🍀
Winey	🍀🍀🍀	Toasty	🍀🍀
Honey	🍀	Smoky	🍀🍀🍀
Creamy	🍀🍀	Earthy	🍀🍀🍀

For those who savour 100% bars, Domori's version, **Il 100%**, is probably as good as it gets. The aromas are forthright – a blend of balsamic notes with earth and woodland, which together make a very clear expression of a cacao plantation. The flavours are challenging because of the unyielding core of cacao, lifted by a bright citrus dart. Fortunately the whole exercise is given charm by Domori's excellent melt, a characteristic of all the bars, and lingering, persistent finish.

El Rey

El Rey are enthusiasts for their chocolate. As Venezuelans, they know that good cacao comes from Venezuela. The business was founded in Caracas in 1929 by José Rafael Tuozzo and Carmelo Zozaya. Realising that they were making the best chocolate in Venezuela, they called it El Rey (The King). Over the years, El Rey has managed to survive various government interventions. It produces a range of single-origin chocolate. The collection from Rio Caribe in north-east Venezuela is interesting. However, the bars made from the Carenero Superior bean in the Barlovento region just east of Caracas are finer and more intense.

El Rey is also particularly proud of its cocoa butter. The usual practice is to strip it of its flavours – a process known as deodorising. Selling off this deodorised product to the cosmetics industry is a profitable aspect of the cacao business. Most chocolate producers, therefore, have to buy in cocoa butter to add to their cocoa liquor, and can typically obtain only the tasteless version.

Enter El Rey's Icoa, a white chocolate made from non-deodorised cocoa butter from Carenero Superior beans. Icoa is named after a goddess of the native people, who was thought to have a white soul. Legend has it that she died crossing Lake Maracaibo on the way to marry a chieftain on the other side. Increasingly, a number of fine chocolate producers – such as Chococo (see page 94) – are using Icoa for their white chocolate.

The Carenero Superior range starts at 41% with the creamy, honeyed **Caoba**. **Bucare** (58.5%) is dark and well-made for those who do not favour bitter chocolate – the finish has coffee, coconut and fudgy notes. **Mijao** (61%) has a bright aromatic lift, and is altogether more polished and creamy. This has the

NAME OF THE BAR *El Rey Gran Saman Carenero Superior*
COCOA SOLIDS, BLEND OR ORIGIN *70% Carenero Superior, Venezuela*
INGREDIENTS *Cocoa liquor, sugar, soy lecithin as an emulsifier, flavoured with natural vanilla*
WEIGHT OF BAR *80g* **BAR MADE** *Barquisimeto, Venezuela*
WEBSITE *www.chocolateselrey.com*
AROMA *Bold aromas of red fruits, dried sour cherries, creamy chocolate, roasted coffee*
TASTE *After the aromas, surprisingly slow to blossom, then brisk citrus acidity arrives to underline a grainy, sandy melt, a blast of savoury cocoa, with woody, toasty notes. Dense, bold, expressive.*

PROFILE

Floral		Nutty	🐛
Fruity	🐛🐛🐛	Spicy	
Winey	🐛🐛	Toasty	🐛🐛🐛
Honey	🐛	Smoky	🐛🐛
Creamy	🐛	Earthy	🐛

curious effect of making it seem like the sweeter chocolate, lower in cocoa solids. This is certainly one for grating over cappuccino or coffee ice cream. **Apamate**, at 73.5% the darkest, is again unexpectedly light. It leaves the memory of a delicately refreshing character, like lime juice squeezed over mango. However, this is masked by an unexpected fudgy richness and undermined slightly by a gritty, grainy texture in the mouth.

Enric Rovira

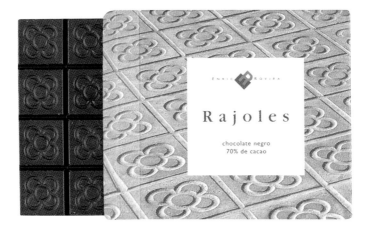

In a world where fine chocolate is being taken increasingly seriously, Enric Rovira is a blast of good humour. His creations always have a visual charm, although they are firmly rooted in classical pastry and chocolate skills, with a modern, technically skilled interpretation. Chocolate is an inherited interest, since his family ran a *pasteleria*, or patisserie. As a child he loved drawing, model-building and, later, film and photography, and he subsequently applied his creative vision to his cakes and to chocolate. When he opened his business in 1993 he called it (in Catalan) Enric Rovira Xocolater de Barcelona; the name is a reference to the skills of Barcelona's chocolatiers in the 1960s and 1970s.

Among Rovira's collections is one inspired by Barcelona's late 19th-century architecture, most famously that of Antoni Gaudí, designer of the Sagrada Familia church in Barcelona. Rovira's chocolate tablets, in small and larger sizes, are called **Rajoles**, modelled on the paving stones designed by Josep Puig i Cadafalch for the Casa Amatller at Paseo de Gracia 41. Amatller was himself a chocolatier, and his Amatllons, chocolate-coated caramelised Spanish almonds, in their period packaging, are a popular souvenir of the city.

NAME OF THE BAR *Enric Rovira Rajoles Chocolate Negro*
COCOA SOLIDS, BLEND OR ORIGIN *70%*
INGREDIENTS *Cacao, sugar, vanilla, soya lecithin*
WEIGHT OF BAR *100g*
BAR MADE *Barcelona, Spain*
WEBSITE *www.enricrovira.com*
AROMA *Deeply favoured, berry and raisin fruit*
TASTE *Starts firm and tough but builds slowly and gently to a well-balanced bar with a fudgy, mildly grainy texture.*

PROFILE

Floral		Nutty	🌟
Fruity		Spicy	🌟
Winey	🌟🌟	Toasty	🌟🌟
Honey	🌟🌟	Smoky	🌟
Creamy	🌟🌟	Earthy	🌟

A recent innovation is **The Making of Chocolate** in conjuction with Claudio Corallo (see page 102). Packed into a circular tin, resembling an old film reel container, is a DVD of Rovira's documentary on Corallo and samples from various stages of the process from beans to bar: beans, cocoa mass and finished chocolate, all from Corallo's plantation on Príncipe.

François Pralus

François Pralus comes from a classic pastry chef background – his father Auguste was a Meilleur Ouvrier de France, the top professional qualification – and as a young man he worked with many well-known names. His first work experience, at Bernachon (see page 82), gave him the idea of sourcing his own cacao beans. He has carried out the research and the transformation of the beans with energy and enthusiasm, and a pleasant leavening of humour.

Typical of this is the Barre Infernale Lait – the 'hellish milk chocolate bar' – a riot of chocolate, hazelnuts and almonds transformed by its name and by its raffia and brown paper wrapper. The theme continues with the São Tomé bar (see facing page) made in conjuction with Claudio Corallo (see page 102), which is bursting with nibs. This is a bar that divides people; I like it for the 75% bitterness leavened by nibs. In Brazil he works with the Badaró family for his Brazilian cacao, and he gave them and Frederick Schilling some help at the outset of AMMA (see page 72). He has long wanted his own plantation, and in 1999 he purchased 27 hectares (67 acres) on the island of Nosy Be off the north-west tip of Madagascar.

For those who are serious about their beans, there is a wide-ranging portfolio of bars from different origins around the world. Each expresses the character of the origin, but also has the typical Pralus signature – a warm, rich roast. All are 75% except the milk version, **Mélissa**, which is 45%. Despite her charming name, she sadly lacks appeal. It is often the case that milk chocolate from top dark chocolatiers disappoints. Better by far is the 80% **Fortissima**, which is, as its name suggests, resoundingly dark, but in the gentlest way. If only more 80% bars were as good as this.

NAME OF THE BAR *François Pralus Djakarta 75%*

COCOA SOLIDS, BLEND OR ORIGIN *75%, Criollo and Trinitario, Djakarta, Indonesia*

INGREDIENTS *Cocoa, sugar, pure cocoa butter, GMO-free soya lecithin*

WEIGHT OF BAR *100g*

BAR MADE *Roanne, Loire, France*

WEBSITE *www.chocolats-pralus.com*

AROMA *Tobacco, earth, toast, citrus*

TASTE *The toasty aroma is matched on the palate. The melt reveals molasses, raisins, toasted coffee. Boldly flavoured but supple texture. Definitely an iron fist in a velvet glove.*

PROFILE

Floral		Nutty	🌿	
Fruity	🌿	Spicy	🌿	
Winey	🌿🌿	Toasty	🌿🌿🌿	
Honey	🌿🌿🌿	Smoky	🌿🌿🌿	
Creamy	🌿🌿	Earthy	🌿🌿	

Galler

Jean Galler is the model of the modern chocolatier as intellectual. With a refined bone
structure, a domed forehead and elegant specta-
cles, this is surely a man who has thought
deeply about chocolate. Galler started his own
business when he was 21 with the assistance of
his family, who were already in the patisserie
business. The empire has expanded steadily,
with boutiques and concessions around the
world. He may be Belgian, yet his approach
to chocolate is less creamy and sweet than
some of his compatriots.

Galler is well-known for his cartoon-
decorated tins of the children's favourite,
Langues de Chat. He is also developing
ranges beyond the usual Belgian classics.
For instance, his Japanese-influenced
Kaori calligraphy box contains
flavoured chocolate sticks and a set of
'ink' pots so that the taster can explore
a range of flavours. An indulgence perhaps, but a step
away from the traditional Belgian full-cream–and-butter extravaganzas.

The bars are colour-coded, foil- and paper-wrapped, solid creations. Fifteen
chunky squares, each embossed with the Galler signature, make up a 100g bar.
The 'Heritage' bars are the house blends at 34%, 70% and 85%. The 'Blended'
range is intended to have the complexity of fine wine blended from different
grape varieties. These bars blend across countries: **Papouasie-Arriba** (Papua
New Guinea) 60%; **São Tomé-Tanzanie** 70%; (see profile facing page) and
Equateur-Saint Domingue (Ecuador-Santo Domingo) 80%. The 70% is the
most successful of these. The 80% is at the same time hollow and bitter; while
the 60% lacks depth although it has a creamy chocolate profile.

NAME OF THE BAR *Galler São Tomé Tanzanie Blended Chocolat Noir 70%*
COCOA SOLIDS, BLEND OR ORIGIN *70%, São Tomé and Tanzania*
INGREDIENTS *Cocoa mass, sugar, cocoa butter, emulsifier soya lecithin, natural vanilla*
WEIGHT OF BAR *100g*
BAR MADE *Chaudfontaine, Maastricht, Belgium*
WEBSITE *www.galler.com*
AROMA *Tobacco, but also floral, with lime blossom*
TASTE *Begins dark, then develops minty notes, with a light, creamy, mocha mid-palate and a firm, tannic signature on the finish.*

PROFILE

Floral		Nutty	🌱
Fruity		Spicy	🌱
Winey		Toasty	🌱🌱
Honey		Smoky	🌱🌱
Creamy	🌱🌱🌱	Earthy	🌱🌱🌱

Ginger Elizabeth

Of all the chocolate samples on my tasting table, these were the ones that disappeared the fastest if I happened to leave the door open. Simple, moulded dark bars, they did not look out of the ordinary but the important thing is that they tasted delicious.

Ginger Elizabeth Hahn was convinced that her future lay in food after a summer course at the Culinary Institute of America when she was 16. After two years of study and a meeting with Julia Child, she won a scholarship from the IACP (International Association of Culinary Professionals). She moved to New York, where she studied and worked for chocolatier Jacques Torres, before moving on to the Ritz-Carlton in Chicago. Finally, in 2005 she set up on her own, aged 24, in Sacramento, California.

Ginger is one of the few chocolatiers to have a 'philosophy' button on her website. She shows herself to be aware of her social responsibility: 'From the farmer to the chocolatiers, much of the chocolate we use has traveled to three continents before it arrives in our shop. It is important for us to respect and understand the roles of all those involved along the way.'

Above the seriousness comes flavour. Try these, for instance: **Crispy Coconut Kaffir Lime Dessert Bar** or **Vanilla Bean Toffee Almond Dessert Bar**. Ginger calls these Dessert Bars 'because the creative process that goes into designing them is very similar to how I approach designing individual pastries and desserts. Everything is hand made and folded into a great couverture chocolate.' These dark bars reveal a fine balance of sweet, salty and bitter as well as crunchy and smooth. She concludes: 'We don't do it just to be different; the end result has to be delicious … and the customer has to want to eat it again (and again, and again …)'

NAME OF THE BAR *Ginger Elizabeth Bittersweet Chocolate 70%*
COCOA SOLIDS, BLEND OR ORIGIN *70%*
INGREDIENTS *Bittersweet chocolate (cocoa beans, sugar, cocoa butter, soya lecithin, vanilla)*
WEIGHT OF BAR *100g*
BAR MADE *Sacramento, California, USA*
WEBSITE *www.gingerelizabeth.com*
AROMA *Delicately, darkly chocolatey*
TASTE *A smooth supple melt reveals a finely balanced blend with echoes of mocha, and red fruit highlights. Long, persistent finish.*

PROFILE

Floral	🌶🌶	Nutty	
Fruity	🌶	Spicy	🌶
Winey	🌶	Toasty	🌶
Honey	🌶🌶	Smoky	
Creamy	🌶🌶	Earthy	🌶

Ginger Elizabeth
CHOCOLATES

Bittersweet Chocolate Bar
70% Cocoa Content

NET WT. 3.5 OZ (100g)

Godiva

For many chocolate lovers, Godiva is the ultimate glamorous chocolatier, with its beautifully presented chocolates. The brightly lit windows of its shops in the snowy streets of Brussels in the run-up to Christmas seem to typify the traditional celebration in that city.

In fact, Godiva dates back only to 1926, when Joseph Draps started the business in Brussels, naming his brand rather daringly after Lady Godiva. His first shop was in the centre of the city, in the Grand Place. His chocolate has since become a byword for the butter-and-cream richness of Belgium's chocolates, also found in brands such as Leonidas and Neuhaus.

Godiva's fame outside Belgium was driven by its purchase in 1972 by the multinational Campbell's Soup company, and further stores and concessions opened up globally. By 2008 Campbell's had decided that Godiva was not core to its business and sold it to Yildiz Holding, a major Turkish food group.

Despite the changes of ownership, Draps' factory in Brussels remains little changed from its beginnings – it has just become larger as the warren of rooms expands. The company still treasures some of its antique equipment, and the development chief still starts his day by tempering chocolate on a slab before experimenting with recipes. The *manons* (chocolates filled with fresh cream and a walnut) are still dipped into a vat of melted sugar by hand by a small number of dextrous ladies, who never seem to lose one in the snowy depths, despite making 60 kilos a day. And the *manons* are just one of an extensive range of ganaches, truffles, pralinés and caramels. However, to feed the global demand there is a second factory in Pennsylvania.

NAME OF THE BAR *Godiva Dark Chocolate 72% Cacao*
COCOA SOLIDS, BLEND OR ORIGIN *72%*
INGREDIENTS *Cocoa mass, sugar, cocoa butter, emulsifier, soya lecithin*
WEIGHT OF BAR *100g*
BAR MADE *Germany; Pennsylvania, USA*
WEBSITE *www.godiva.be; www.godiva.com*
AROMA *Earthy, smoky, mocha*
TASTE *A rich, mouthfilling approach to dark chocolate: starts nutty, builds through notes of liquorice to a very persistent finish with coffee highlights.*

PROFILE

Floral		Nutty	🌶🌶
Fruity	🌶	Spicy	🌶
Winey		Toasty	🌶
Honey	🌶🌶🌶	Smoky	🌶
Creamy	🌶🌶🌶	Earthy	🌶

Bars have never had a high profile in the range, but recently Godiva has been catching up with contemporary trends. The new slim bars are a promising development. As well as the classic Belgian dark bar (see profile above), there is a 72% **Dark Chocolate with Almonds**. Inside it has the appearance of salami with its minced white almonds, which stick a little in the teeth. The 31% milk bar is caramel coloured and caramel in flavour, sweet and supple with a cloying finish. The 85% **Santo Domingo** is very dark and brisk, but like all the other dark bars in the range has a good, clean finish.

Green & Black's

Craig Sams is the first to admit that he knew little about chocolate when he started in 1991. Sams' background was in macrobiotic and organic foods; he co-founded the Whole Earth brand in the United Kingdom. It was his partner, now his wife, the journalist Josephine Fairley, who spotted the potential of the chocolate sample on his desk, sent by a supplier in Togo. The couple launched their own organic 70% bar. This was followed three years later by the spicy (cinnamon and nutmeg), citrussy (orange and vanilla) **Maya Gold**, inspired by a Belize drink called Kukuh and the first product in the United Kingdom to win Fairtrade status. It was a risky choice for a new company as it is a flavour that rouses strong opinions. I am one of its fans.

In 2005 Green & Black's was purchased by Cadbury Schweppes, and Sams is now President. The 'sell-out' caused much debate and the result has been to begin to turn Green & Black's into a global brand. With this Cadbury (now Kraft) investment, Green & Black's has the marketing muscle to become the world leader in organic and Fairtrade chocolate. The entire production is organic, mainly sourced from the Dominican Republic, while Belize has been supplying Fairtrade cacao. Some 15 years on from the launch of **Maya Gold**, the company finally declared in 2010 that it would become 100% Fairtrade by the end of 2011. New investment is also supporting Green & Black's diversification into biscuits, ice creams,

NAME OF THE BAR *Green and Black's Organic Dark 70%*

COCOA SOLIDS, BLEND OR ORIGIN *70%, Trinitario*

INGREDIENTS *Organic cocoa mass, organic raw cane sugar, organic cocoa butter, soya lecithin, organic vanilla extract, organic whole milk powder*

WEIGHT OF BAR *100g*

BAR MADE *Italy*

WEBSITE *www.greenandblacks.com*

AROMA *Bold, dark aromas, with balsamic, earthy, smoky notes and a lift of white flowers*

TASTE *The melt is fudgy and grainy; the flavours start dark, with citrus lights, then power through to a firm, tannic finish. Long and insistent with an acidic bite.*

PROFILE

Floral		Nutty	🍫🍫
Fruity	🍫🍫	Spicy	
Winey	🍫	Toasty	🍫🍫
Honey	🍫	Smoky	🍫🍫
Creamy		Earthy	🍫🍫🍫

Easter eggs and more. By bringing organic, Fairtrade chocolate into the mainstream, perhaps 'sustainability' and 'ethics' will become more palatable.

What of the chocolate? The dark bar itself is tannic and at its best in the version filled with mint fondant. The cherries in the 60% bar, like the currants in the hazelnut bar, only emphasise the sourness of the chocolate. Green & Black's real success is with its flavoured milk bars: sweet and milky, and cleverly flavoured with butterscotch or almonds.

By the way, there never was a Mr Green or a Ms Black – Sams and Fairley made up the names, which sound suitably sustainable and dark and chocolatey.

The Grenada Chocolate Company

If Amedei's is the prettiest factory in the world (see page 70), Grenada's is definitely the most colourful, with an energy found throughout the business, across the website and over the chocolate wrappers themselves. The Grenada Chocolate Company was set up in 1999 with the idea of creating an organic cocoa farmers' and chocolate-makers' co-operative. Its original aim is simply and powerfully put: 'to revolutionise the cocoa-chocolate system that typically keeps cocoa production separate from chocolate-making and therefore takes advantage of cocoa farmers. We believe that the cocoa farmers should benefit as much as the chocolate-makers.'

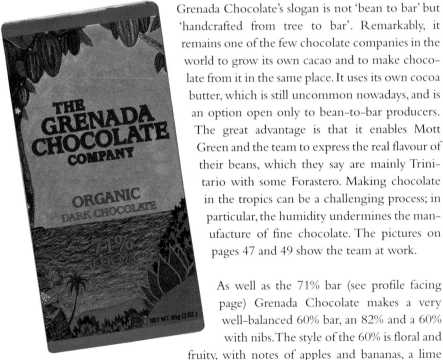

Grenada Chocolate's slogan is not 'bean to bar' but 'handcrafted from tree to bar'. Remarkably, it remains one of the few chocolate companies in the world to grow its own cacao and to make chocolate from it in the same place. It uses its own cocoa butter, which is still uncommon nowadays, and is an option open only to bean-to-bar producers. The great advantage is that it enables Mott Green and the team to express the real flavour of their beans, which they say are mainly Trinitario with some Forastero. Making chocolate in the tropics can be a challenging process; in particular, the humidity undermines the manufacture of fine chocolate. The pictures on pages 47 and 49 show the team at work.

As well as the 71% bar (see profile facing page) Grenada Chocolate makes a very well-balanced 60% bar, an 82% and a 60% with nibs. The style of the 60% is floral and fruity, with notes of apples and bananas, a lime daiquiri even. Surely that is the splash of the sea in the background? As a

NAME OF THE BAR *The Grenada Chocolate Company Organic Dark Chocolate 71%*
COCOA SOLIDS, BLEND OR ORIGIN *71%, Grenada, organic*
INGREDIENTS *Organic cocoa beans, organic cane sugar, organic cocoa butter,*
emulsifier: organic soya lecithin, organic vanilla beans
WEIGHT OF BAR *85g*
BAR MADE *St Patrick's, Grenada, The Caribbean*
WEBSITE *www.grenadachocolate.com*
AROMA *Earthy, red fruit, notes of vanilla*
TASTE *Big and bold with a punchy, citrus component. The freshness arrives instantly; the fudgy, mildly grainy melt reveals roasted mocha and toast, with liquorice and grassy highlights. Very long.*

PROFILE

Floral			Nutty	
Fruity	🍫🍫🍫		Spicy	
Winey	🍫🍫		Toasty	🍫🍫
Honey	🍫🍫		Smoky	🍫🍫
Creamy	🍫		Earthy	🍫🍫🍫

tasting note this is fanciful, but it emphasises the contrast with the roasted darkness of the 71%.

The company puts the bold flavours down to the Caribbean island's rich volcanic soils. The processing (or relative lack of it) also makes a difference. While the bars are smooth, they have not been refined out of their lives. In a small-scale study for the Academy of Chocolate, the Grenada 71% came out higher in antioxidants than other bars with similar cocoa solids. The test was too small to have statistical significance but it confirmed a general assumption that less refined chocolate contains more antioxidants.

Guido Gobino

Guido Gobino's chocolate speaks for itself. There's a purity in the flavour, as well as a deliciousness that talks of pure pleasure. The man himself is charmingly moustachioed, and his playfulness is cheerfully illustrated on a merry tour of the factory hosted by a Willy Wonka character who meets Guido and his team (you can watch it on You Tube *http://www.youtube.com/watch?v=SNbfRryn3bg*). It appears to be a world away from the academic approach of some other chocolate producers, yet beneath his humour Gobino's approach to fine ingredients is just as serious.

Guido Gobino's business is based in Turin, so chocolates made with Piedmontese hazelnuts (*gianduja*) figure strongly. *Gianduja*, a sumptuous blend of ground roasted hazelnuts with chocolate, was the clever solution to the shortage of cacao in the 1860s during Italy's wars of independence – local hazelnuts were added to extend the chocolate. Gobino's collection includes a typical **Giandujotto**, made with milk and cocoa butter, and a less creamy, more traditional version, **Tourinot**, with chocolate, sugar and hazelnuts.

I first encountered Gobino's craftsmanship when judging at the 2008 Academy of Chocolate Awards. He submitted an item of extreme simplicity: **Cremino**, a little cube, measuring 2 x 2 x 1.5cm, of *gianduja* paste, with sea salt and Ligurian extra virgin olive oil. In the mouth it blossomed into a silky paste, enhanced by the supple oil, a light crunch of hazelnuts, and then a swirl of sea salt to lift and calm the sweetness. The size perfectly matched the richness of the contents. It won a deserved Gold.

NAME OF THE BAR APPEARANCE *Guido Gobino Extra Bitter 70%*
COCOA SOLIDS, BLEND OR ORIGIN *70%*
INGREDIENTS *Cocoa, sugar, cocoa butter, natural extract of Bourbon vanilla, emulsifier: soya lecithin (GMO free)*
WEIGHT OF BAR *60g*
BAR MADE *Turin, Piedmont, Italy*
WEBSITE *www.guidogobino.it*
AROMA *Liquorice, earthy, creamily chocolatey*
TASTE *A dark, earthy, roasted profile, with liquorice and herbs. The flavour builds rapidly to a savoury mid-palate, then falls gradually away.*

PROFILE

Floral		Nutty	
Fruity		Spicy	🌶
Winey		Toasty	🌶🌶🌶
Honey	🌶🌶🌶	Smoky	🌶🌶
Creamy	🌶🌶🌶	Earthy	🌶🌶

Gobino's business is not just about making chocolate, but also about savouring it. His shop in Turin offers the city's favourite coffee, the *bicerin* (a layered drink of espresso coffee, drinking chocolate and milk), alongside chocolates, but also has an 'extreme tasting' room, with audio and video installations to add to the experience. As well as a 35% milk bar and dark bars at 60%, 70% and 80%, there are **Cialdina** discs in a range of blends, origins and intriguing flavours.

A particular curiosity is **Egizia**, his representation of ancient Egypt. It is an 85% blend of cacao from Java and Trinidad with muscovado sugar, sea salt and myrrh extract. Balsamic and treacly at the outset, with a grainy texture, the bitterness softens and the flavours linger well.

Guittard

These days, when chocolate is dominated by global brands, Guittard has some reason to feel pleased with its achievements. Launched in San Francisco by Frenchman Etienne Guittard in 1868, Guittard is the oldest family chocolate business still operating in the United States. Until the recent blossoming of artisan bean-to-bar producers, it was one of a very small number of producers to work directly with growers.

Gary Guittard (President and CEO since 1989) has had to keep up with changing palates. On the one hand, there is the regular demand for creamy, comforting milkiness in chocolate. On the other hand there is the growing band of dark chocolate aficionados. This is where Quetzalcoatl bar (see profile facing page), with no added cocoa butter, is intended to find a niche.

Guittard keeps in touch with new sources. For example, the Waialua Estate in Hawaii is currently sending its cacao to Guittard to be processed. This estate was an interesting project set up by Dole (the pineapple people) who were investigating other forms of agriculture. Dole sourced and planted some top cacaos from around the world. Hawaiian cacao has grabbed the attention of some small producers in the United States, partly because of its proximity to the US mainland. However, as with all origins it is important to remember

NAME OF THE BAR *E. Guittard Quetzalcoatl 72%*

COCOA SOLIDS, BLEND OR ORIGIN *72% cocoa mass 'contains no added cocoa butter'; Anillo del Fuego Blended Chocolate: a blend from 'cacao growing regions in the ring of fire' around the world.*

INGREDIENTS *Cacao beans, pure cane sugar, soya lecithin, vanilla beans*

WEIGHT OF BAR *2oz*

BAR MADE *Burlingame, California, USA*

WEBSITE *www.guittard.com*

AROMA *Raspberries, redcurrants, coconut*

TASTE *The aromas reappear as flavours, with a creamy richness to mask the darkness. Back notes of pepper arrive, with a lift of citrus, ending in a long sweet finish. The texture is lightly grainy and fudgy.*

PROFILE

Floral		Nutty	✿✿✿
Fruity	✿✿	Spicy	✿
Winey		Toasty	✿
Honey	✿✿	Smoky	
Creamy	✿✿✿	Earthy	

that the taste of the cacao will be influenced by the technique and flavours of the producer.

Guittard's is a classic range in tune with its classic packaging and the brand mission of 'vintage chocolate making in the French tradition'. The chocolate is well-finished with small chunky squares with a fine sheen, a soft melt and an echo of sweetness. The bars have romantic names, redolent of lost empires. **Orinoco** 38% is milky with what Guittard describes as its signature cinnamon note; **Tsaratana** 61% is semisweet, soothed by its sweetness; **Quetzalcoatl** (above) is named after the Mexican feathered serpent god; **Nocturne** 91% manages to retain the Guittard softness, unlike the chalky approach typical of bars of this strength. There are also four origin bars, all at 65%: **Sur del Lago** (Venezuela), **Quevedo** (Ecuador), **Chucuri** (Colombia) and **Ambanja** (Madagascar). Given their stylistic similarity they are a good way to carry out an introductory tasting about chocolate origins.

Haigh's

The Haigh family are coming up to their first century. They began their business in 1915 with a shop in Adelaide selling sweets and ice creams – an ideal combination with a ticket to the new silent films. After the Second World War, the third generation, John Haigh, went to work at Lindt & Sprüngli (see page 156) to learn all about chocolate, and he also spent time travelling to pick up new ideas for sales and marketing. Haigh's kept up their association with the cinema, and generations of Australians bought Haigh's chocolates from trays in front of the screen during the interval. However, in the 1960s, when more people stayed at home to watch television, the business had to adapt. The Haighs chose to expand their business to Melbourne, and subsequently also to Sydney.

They use cacao from Ecuador, Papua New Guinea and African origins, and manage the roasting and blending in Adelaide. In a nation with a shortage of water, the company is committed to conserving water and energy in the factory, and rainwater is converted into steam for factory usage.

The bars themselves are wrapped in a cellophane bag, closed with a sticker, and then packed in a cardboard case. The milk chocolate at 36% is very smooth with a good melt, and a light caramel character. There are three flavoured bars, all milk at 36%. The **Peppermint** is very dominant and the **Orange** sweetly fruity. The **Milk Coffee Chocolate** is the most successful – it has all the traditional character of a Swiss coffee shop.

NAME OF THE BAR *Haigh's Gourmet Dark Chocolate*
COCOA SOLIDS, BLEND OR ORIGIN *70%, 'a unique blend of premium
South American and African cocoa beans'*
INGREDIENTS *Cocoa solids (cocoa mass, cocoa butter), sugar, soya lecithin, vanilla, milk*
WEIGHT OF BAR *100g*
BAR MADE *Adelaide, South Australia*
WEBSITE *www.haighschocolates.com.au*
AROMA *Vanilla, roast caramel, light notes of chocolate*
TASTE *A slow, smooth melt, with a fudge, caramel, dairy profile, slowly revealing a deep, high-
roast bitterness and a long, drying finish with a grip of tannin, lifted by a dart of citrus.*

PROFILE

Floral		Nutty	🌶
Fruity	🌶🌶	Spicy	
Winey		Toasty	🌶🌶
Honey	🌶🌶	Smoky	🌶🌶
Creamy	🌶🌶	Earthy	🌶

Right: The famous Beehive Corner
building is one of the sights of old
Adelaide. Haigh's Chocolates has been
located here for over a century.

Hotel Chocolat

Angus Thirlwell is an entrepreneur and enthusiast, with close connections to the Caribbean. He and his colleagues at Hotel Chocolat started up in the days before internet shopping and first built up their company through mail order catalogues and a tasting club. Regular score sheets from members were an invaluable form of market research. The tasting club now has 100,000 members, who are offered a selection of new chocolates each month.

Hotel Chocolat now has more than 40 shops in the United Kingdom, Boston, USA, and Bahrain, Dubai and Kuwait in the Middle East, as well as a portfolio of private and cor- porate consumers. Products are carefully segmented in the best marketing manner, by occasion, style, person and price, so it is very clear to customers – in the shops, the catalogue or on the website – how they can spoil themselves or treat others. Hotel Chocolat makes a feature of generous portions, apparently irregularly shaped and unevenly decorated. For example the Extra Thick Easter Egg is a clever response to consumers' disappointment about the fact that many chocolate egg shells are thinner than they used to be. Hotel Choco- lat's main business is the popular collections of boxed chocolates, although their flamboyantly decorated giant slabs are certainly eyecatching.

Since 2006, with the purchase of the Rabot Estate near the Piton mountains on St Lucia, Hotel Chocolat can call itself 'British chocolatier and cocoa grower' selling bars under the 'Purist' label. There is a hotel opening on the estate, promising chocolate therapy as well as walks among the trees. A 'Rabot Estate' shop has opened in London's fashionable Borough Market, enabling

NAME OF THE BAR *Hotel Chocolat The Purist Single Estate Dark 72%*
COCOA SOLIDS, BLEND OR ORIGIN *72%, Rabot Estate, St Lucia, West Indies*
INGREDIENTS *Cocoa mass, cocoa butter, cane sugar*
WEIGHT OF BAR *75g*
BAR MADE *Royston, Cambridgeshire, England*
WEBSITE *www.hotelchocolat.co.uk*
AROMA *Earth, red wine, redcurrants*
TASTE *Lively character of red fruits opens up to savoury, textured roast, with a full palate and light grip of tannin on the finish.*

PROFILE

Floral		Nutty	❦❦
Fruity	❦❦❦	Spicy	❦
Winey	❦❦	Toasty	❦❦❦
Honey	❦❦	Smoky	❦❦ ❦
Creamy		Earthy	❦

Hotel Chocolat to introduce the idea of seasonality and ethical production into a high street brand. The bars and the packaging are changing as the team fine-tunes the production, testing out conching times as long as 120 hours. They buy cacao from other island growers as well as from their own estate.

New to the range are the St Lucia 50% **Dash of Milk**, 70% **Dash of Milk** and two 65% dark bars, one conched

Above: The Pitons in south-west St Lucia.

for 96 hours and one for 120 hours – these make a fascinating contrast. The '96' is wilder and bolder while the '120' is more supple and fine. The Purist range also includes 80%, 90% and 100% bars from Hacienda Iara in Ecuador, 65% from Alto El Sol in Peru and 70% from Chuao in Venezuela.

Jean-Paul Hévin

A visit to a Hévin tea-room gives you a glimpse of Parisian elegance. The riot of classical pastries, such as 'Choco Passion', 'Marquise' and 'Feuilletine praliné', demonstrate exceptional technical skill. Hévin won the chefs' highest accolade of Meilleur Ouvrier de France for pastry and confectionery in 1986, and he has a skilled team servicing his shops in Paris, Japan and Hong Kong, and his mail order business.

The packaging is as discreet and elegant as his chocolate: there are no wild shocks or rough corners in his creations. There may be some surprises, particularly when he uses cheese with chocolate, but even this he manages to handle convincingly, because of his technical skill. He blends Epoisses with cumin, and Pont l'Evêque with thyme, and suggests trying them with a sweet Vin Doux Naturel (a fortified wine from southern France).

In acknowledgement of its location, the shop on Avenue de la Motte Picquet sells a chocolate Eiffel Tower. This must be the only one in the city that declares its cocoa solids (64%). Usually these items are made out of cheap chocolate; Hévin's is the real deal. The most impressive of his artifices is, appropriately enough for one of the world centres of haute couture, a chocolate stiletto-heeled shoe: '9.9cm heel, size 35, right foot only, €54.10', representing, apparently, '160g of true happiness'.

Hévin ships more or less worldwide. While placing an order, take a look at his 'energy bars'. These are not the usual blends of cereal and seeds, but instead are chocolate bars flavoured with

NAME OF THE BAR *Jean-Paul Hévin*

COCOA SOLIDS, BLEND OR ORIGIN *64%, Papouasie (Papua New Guinea),*
Forastero and Trinitario

INGREDIENTS *Cocoa mass, sugar, cocoa butter, emulsifier: soya lecithin*

WEIGHT OF BAR *75g*

BAR MADE *Paris, France*

WEBSITE *www.jphevin.com*

AROMA *Floral with red fruits, notes of sweet spice and mocha*

TASTE *Starts richly creamy with flavours of pure, clean chocolate, followed by a lingering lift of lime. Richer notes appear of caramel and chocolate cake. Long delicate finish with refined tannin.*

PROFILE

Floral	🌱🌱	Nutty	🌱
Fruity	🌱🌱🌱	Spicy	
Winey	🌱🌱	Toasty	🌱
Honey	🌱🌱🌱	Smoky	
Creamy	🌱	Earthy	🌱

ginger, chilli, Tonka bean and Szechuan pepper, all known for their stimulating, energising properties. Gym fanatics will be charmed by the humour of his sugar-free 'abdominal bars', called **Pecs**, **Muscle**, **Curl** and **Fitness**, moulded like impressive sets of pectoral muscles, to give you 'effortlessly ... a crisp, dream body'.

There are some flavoured bars, but the focus is on plain house blends – 76%, 80% and 81% – and origins. There are 11 general origins – such as Venezuela, Ecuador, Java – and four specific 'exceptional' ones, including Papua New Guinea (profiled above) and Chuao. Hévin is a *fondeur* – in other words, he does not make his own chocolate. However, he gives plenty of information about origins on his website for those who are interested.

He has sage advice about how best to enjoy a chocolate bar: 'I enjoy a few squares, served at room temperature, towards the end of the morning to replenish my energy sources. Then I have a few more squares as a dessert after my meal. During the afternoon I like to eat chocolate with bread and butter, whereas in the evening, I prefer just to let a square melt right under my palate.'

Kallari

This is one of the rare bean-to-bar producers that ticks (nearly) all the boxes. Nearly? More of that below. Kallari (meaning 'to begin' or 'the early times') comes from Ecuador and the cacao is grown and fermented by a co-operative of 850 indigenous Kichwa farmers in the Amazon region. They make their own bars in a purpose-built factory in Quito. By controlling the chain of production, they earn the income which in the typical model of cacao production is lost to the middle men. Furthermore they have no need of Fairtrade certification – or of paying for the certification – since the way they work more than benefits the whole community already.

Their path has been eased by a number of expert visitors: a US volunteer suggested they focus on their native cacao; the late Robert Steinberg, one of the founders of Scharffen Berger (see page 200), took their rare Nacional beans to Slow Food in Turin in 2004, where they were accepted into the Presidium of heirloom varieties. Next came Swiss chocolatier Felchlin, who in 2005 advised them on the quality of the beans required in fermentation. In 2006 the Canadian chocolatier Eric Gilbert taught the Kallari staff about chocolate making and tempering, and the growers were granted organic status. Importantly, through these external influences, Kallari learnt what fine chocolate was about – a step that many growers, used to tasting just local confectionery, find difficult.

NAME OF THE BAR *Kallari 70% Cacao Single Source Organic Chocolate*
COCOA SOLIDS, BLEND OR ORIGIN *70%, Ecuador*
INGREDIENTS *Rainforest Alliance Certified organic cocoa mass, organic cane sugar, organic cocoa butter, organic whole vanilla bean*
WEIGHT OF BAR *70g*
BAR MADE *Quito, Ecuador*
WEBSITE *www.kallari.com*
AROMA *Creamy, nutty, floral, suggesting a milkier chocolate*
TASTE *The melt is slow, and the flavours develop just as slowly; bitterness and tobacco come through underneath the cream, then a grainy texture as of overbaked cake crust develops, on the verge of being too bitter. The finish is dry and a little tannic but softened by an unexpected buttery sweetness.*

PROFILE

Floral		Nutty	❦❦	
Fruity	❦❦	Spicy	❦	
Winey	❦	Toasty	❦❦	
Honey	❦	Smoky	❦❦	
Creamy	❦❦	Earthy	❦	

Kallari already had their own shade-grown Nacional cacao, a version of Forastero found in Ecuador and one of the highly prized fine flavour cacaos, along with a selection of Trinitarios and Criollos. Their raw material was good.

What they needed next was a business structure. The fairy godfather was Steve McDonnell, founder of Applegate Farms, the US organic meat company. He founded the Kallari Chocolate Company in the United States, all of whose profits return to the community. In 2008, production in their new factory began in earnest.

What of the chocolate? This is where the 'nearly' comes in. The finish is good, only a little scuffed at the edges, a little lacking in sheen. The 70% seems a little lighter than one would expect; the 75% has a more satisfactory balance. The 85% has a wilder, plantation character, and the batch I tasted for this book had an earthiness as if of faulty beans. Overall it is a great start; I am sure that Kallari can make chocolate that scores on taste not just ethics.

Kaoka

Behind the organic and fair trade Kaoka label lie more than two decades of work by the Frenchman André Deberdt. He started out in Togo, working on programmes for organically grown tropical fruits. He soon developed an interest in cacao, and initiated a project to export fermented dried cacao. The chocolate was first made in France, and its quality was quickly recognised. This was also the origin of the Green & Black's brand, which was launched in the United Kingdom in 1991 (see page 128).

Over the following years Deberdt sourced cacao from other origins, including Papua New Guinea and Madagascar, while also building his own brand in France. In 1998 the relationship with Green & Black's came to an end. Kaoka has contined to grow as a brand and now sources organic cacao from Ecuador, São Tomé and Príncipe, Vanuatu, the Dominican Republic and Venezuela.

Kaoka produces couverture for chefs and patissiers, as well as bars. The bars are large, slim rectangles, similar in shape to a Lindt bar. There are plain bars at 36%, 55% and 70% (see profile facing page) and an 80% **Ecuador**. This is impressively dark with a good sheen and aromas that leap out: balsamic, floral, red fruits and tar. The snap is excellent – appetisingly crisp. The texture, however, is disappointingly sludgy after the freshness of the snap. However,

NAME OF THE BAR *Kaoka Noir 70% Organic Dark Chocolate*
COCOA SOLIDS, BLEND OR ORIGIN *70%, blend of Ecuador, São Tomé,*
organic, fair trade
INGREDIENTS *Organic cocoa mass, organic raw cane sugar, emulsifier: sunflower lecithin,*
organic vanilla extract
WEIGHT OF BAR *100g*
BAR MADE *Tinchebray, Orne, France*
WEBSITE *www.kaoka.fr*
AROMA *Red fruits, floral, creamy*
TASTE *Immediately nutty, with high toast mocha notes; firm tannins follow on with bitter,*
woody, earthy notes. Finishes wih a lift of citrus. A bold, dark bar.

PROFILE

Floral		Nutty	🍫🍫
Fruity	🍫🍫	Spicy	🍫
Winey		Toasty	🍫🍫🍫
Honey		Smoky	🍫🍫🍫
Creamy	🍫🍫	Earthy	🍫🍫🍫

the flavours are bold, with citrus acidity, toasted nuts and tobacco edged by red fruits, with the overall power typical of Ecuador.

Of the flavoured bars, the 55% **Noir Orange** with natural orange extract is sweetly fruity, though the cocoa and the orange do sit apart from each other; much more successful is the 61% **Noir Éclats de Fèves de Cacao Caramelisés**, which has roasted caramelised nibs that stick in the teeth pleasantly, and is perfectly balanced. The raw cane sugar here adds an appealing dark coarseness. The 66% **Noir aux Éclats de Noisettes Caramelisées** (with caramelised hazelnuts, and chocolate from São Tomé and Príncipe) is a clever blend, since the sweet nuts hide the acidity of the chocolate and mask the tannins in the finish.

In all, the flavourings are sensitively chosen and are a lesson in how to add commercial appeal to the sometimes challenging characters of certain cacaos.

Kennedy & Wilson

The most obvious similarity between chocolate and wine is that both are fermented products, with complex flavours that depend on their origins and method of processing. So it is not surprising that a winemaker should become a chocolatier. Peter Wilson, 'one-time punk band manager and bloodbank worker', was a winemaker for the visionary pioneer Dr Bailey Carrodus at the top wine estate Yarra Yering, in the Yarra Valley outside Melbourne in Victoria, Australia.

On a work trip through Europe in 1993, Wilson found himself in Beaune, the centre of the Burgundy wine industry. Hungry for chocolate, he bought a bar of Valrhona chocolate; this was his 'Eureka!' moment. He recognised the chocolate to be as fine and as carefully made as the wines at Yarra Yering.

He was inspired to set up a fine chocolate business at home in Australia with his partner Juliana Kennedy, the business brains of K&W. It took them time to source the equipment, as well as the ingredients. Wilson's technical background, and understanding of flavour, was undoubtedly a help. The business started in 1996, and now also employs the wonderfully moustachioed French patissier/chocolatier, Didier Cadinot.

The chocolates show their European inspiration, with *langues de chat*

NAME OF THE BAR *Kennedy & Wilson Dark Chocolate*
COCOA SOLIDS, BLEND OR ORIGIN *70%, 'made in Australia from the finest imported and local ingredients'*
INGREDIENTS *Cocoa liquor, sugar, cocoa butter, soy lecithin, vanilla*
WEIGHT OF BAR *100g*
BAR MADE *Coldstream, Victoria, Australia*
WEBSITE *www.kennedyandwilson.com.au*
AROMA *Roasted aromas with notes of mint and coconut*
TASTE *The flavour builds gently, from mild caramel creaminess, through a cool menthol freshness and a tang of bitterness. A little hollow in the mid-palate; finishing in a rich, fudgy melt.*

PROFILE

Floral		Nutty	🍦🍦
Fruity	🍦	Spicy	
Winey		Toasty	🍦🍦
Honey	🍦🍦🍦	Smoky	🍦🍦
Creamy	🍦🍦🍦	Earthy	🍦

(cats' tongues), bears and ducks, as well as thins. The filled chocolate range is equally traditional but under the influence of Cadinot is developing flavourings and fillings using local fruits such as raspberries and pears. K&W make flavoured couvertures for restaurants, including 'dark chocolate with tea rose' and 'milk chocolate with cardamom'.

The bars come in glossy boxes: there are two plain bars: the dark (above) and the 48% milk. The milk bar is well finished with a good sheen. It is not too sweet and has an appealing note of coffee. However, it has a fudgy melt and lacks real freshness. The two flavoured bars, **Dark Mint** and **Dark Orange**, are very strong at present, and would benefit from being made more subtle.

Once a winemaker, always a winemaker. With a chocolatier now established on the team, Peter Wilson has joined up with his brother James, a former chemical engineer-turned-winemaker, to launch K&W Wines, from vines grown on the cool southern side of Victoria's Great Dividing Range. Rated one of Australia's best ten new wineries in 2008 by James Halliday, Australia's best-known wine critic, K&W produce Cabernet Sauvignon-Merlot, Chardonnay, Pinot Noir, Shiraz and Semillon.

Kraš

The easiest way to reach the historic old town in Zagreb, the capital city of Croatia, is to take a quick trip up on the funicular railway. Before boarding, drop in for a coffee at the branch of Kraš down the hill on the other side of the main road. If you can find a seat, that is. For the café belonging to Croatia's largest chocolate company is extremely popular.

The original chocolate business was founded in Zagreb in 1911 and the company was then known as Union. It was the first chocolate maker in south-east Europe, and became a supplier to the Imperial Austro-Hungarian court. In 1950, Union merged with other biscuit and confectionery manufacturers. The new business was named Kraš – according to the company history 'after an anti-fascist fighter and a distinguished leader of the workers' movement of the time'. In 1992, Kraš moved from state ownership to private. On privatisation all employees were offered one share and today the management and the employees together own 50 per cent of the business (which continues to make confectionery and biscuits as well as chocolate).

Croatia's population is less than five million, so Kraš needs to look to export markets as well as its domestic one. In Soviet times, its exports to Russia and eastern Europe were

NAME OF THE BAR *Kraš 1911, 77%*
COCOA SOLIDS, BLEND OR ORIGIN *77% Ghana*
INGREDIENTS *Cocoa mass, sugar, cocoa butter, emulsifier soya lecithin E322, natural flavour (vanilla)*
WEIGHT OF BAR *70g*
BAR MADE *Zagreb, Croatia*
WEBSITE *www.kras.hr*
AROMA *Redcurrant and red plum, floral with mint*
TASTE *Dark, bitter flavours rapidly overlaying a rich, fudgy melt. The mid-palate is leafy and toasted with roasted mocha notes. Lingering finish with a light grip of tannin.*

PROFILE

Floral		Nutty	🌰🌰
Fruity		Spicy	🌰🌰
Winey	🌰	Toasty	🌰🌰🌰
Honey	🌰🌰	Smoky	🌰🌰🌰
Creamy	🌰	Earthy	🌰🌰

strong. Today, as Western brands penetrate eastern Europe, Kraš is working to extend its exports into the United States, Canada and Australia. Croatian expats are particularly sentimental about the **Griotte** brand of dark chocolate-coated cherries in liqueur, and **Bajadera**, a chocolate and almond confection.

The 1911 range is the 'serious' fine chocolate brand, with bars in four levels of cocoa solids: milk, 60%, 77% (profiled above) and 88%. There are also three flavours: hazelnut, orange and lemon. The most satisfactory of the bars is the 60%, which has a deep coffee character with a dash of milk. Just the bar to take up into the old town.

L'Artigiano di Gardini

There is no shortage of fine chocolatiers in Italy. Brothers Fabio and Manuele Gardini learned the pleasures of artisan production from their parents, who ran a bakery business. In the last two decades, working as chocolatiers, the brothers have developed an individual style and are more ambitious than most Italian chocolatiers when it comes to adding flavours to their chocolate.

Their speciality is chocolate flavoured with the local 'sweet' sea salt of Cervia, near Ravenna on the Adriatic Coast, which was first enjoyed by the Etruscans. It is collected from the salt pans, and is described as sweet (*dolce*) because of its high levels of sodium chloride (97 per cent) compared to industrially produced 'bitter' salts. Nowadays, when salted milk chocolate and caramels have become so fashionable, it is interesting to taste the work of producers who have a longer tradition in pairing chocolate and salt. It is an undoubtedly salty chocolate – the salt takes centre stage. In a lyrical commentary on their website the Gardinis comment that this flavour combination will remind consumers of 'childhood memories of bread and chocolate and games near the sea'.

The brothers also use Cervia salt in a 38% milk chocolate bar with liquorice, and another at 38% with the local olive oil from Brisighella. Their work with Italian ingredients does not stop there. There are **Il Forlivese** pralines made with Passito (Italian wine made with dried grapes), with mostarda di Cesena, a spicy traditional condiment, and with a blend of pungent Fossa cheese (matured by being buried in a pit for several months) and Passito.

NAME OF THE BAR *L'Artigiano di Gardini Cru Ocumare Extra Fondente*
COCOA SOLIDS, BLEND OR ORIGIN *70%, Criollo from Venezuela*
INGREDIENTS *Cocoa mass, sugar, cocoa butter, emulsifier: soya lecithin*
WEIGHT OF BAR *50g*
BAR MADE *Forlì, Emilia-Romagna, Italy*
WEBSITE *www.lartigianoforli.it*
AROMA *Earthy, with red fruits*
TASTE *An all-Italian cup of cappuccino: the flavours take off slowly, revealing a surprisingly soft milkiness with a refreshing hit of bitterness. Tannin comes in at the finish.*

PROFILE

Floral		Nutty	🍃🍃
Fruity		Spicy	🍃🍃
Winey	🍃	Toasty	🍃🍃
Honey	🍃🍃	Smoky	🍃
Creamy	🍃	Earthy	🍃🍃

Among their more classic creations, the Gardinis make house blend bars at 62%, 70%, 85% and 100%, and a range of milk bars at 32%, 42% and a 'bitter milk' at 52%. They also produce 'Cru' bars from specific estates which include **Ecuador** 73%, **São Tomé**, **Cuba**, and **Ocumare** (see profile above) 70%, and **Madagascar** and **Peru** at 64%.

Their flavoured bars include one made with Venezuelan cocoa nibs, another with Guatemalan Arabica coffee, a 70% São Tomé filled with orange purée, and a 70% Ocumare with rhubarb and citrus. Their range of spiced bars includes 34% star anise, 38% lavender and 54% liquorice.

La Maison du Chocolat

Robert Linxe is a 20th-century chocolate hero. He built a specialist career as a chocolatier, opened a shop in Paris dedicated to fine chocolate and in the 1970s he was at the vanguard of developing origin chocolates. Unlike many chocolatiers of the time he took the bean as seriously as the fillings by collaborating with Valrhona (see page 216) to make his own special blends of couvertures. He now has shops and a loyal following in New York, Tokyo, Hong Kong and London, as well as in Paris and Cannes, and his classical approach to chocolate retailing has been as influential and as imitated as his chocolates themselves.

Linxe is a Basque from the south-west of France, and over the years the Basque country – in both France and Spain – has given rise to a number of leading chefs. At the age of 18, he chose to train as a patissier–chocolatier, and started on the traditional lengthy journey to the top in this most demanding section of the culinary world. He studied in Bayonne, south-west France and then in Switzerland, before finally taking over a patissier–chocolaterie shop in Paris. In 1977, he opened up his first chocolaterie under the name La Maison du Chocolat, in the premises of a former wine merchant in the fashionable Rue du Faubourg St Honoré. The cool cellars were ideal for making chocolate, although with the growth in the business the factory has subsequently moved out of the centre of Paris.

La Maison's shops are sumptuously chocolatey in colour and content. It is a tribute to Linxe's skill that many of his original creations remain popular, and that the shapes and styles he created 30 years ago are still up to date. His bars have alluring names, which speak of cacao's origins – **Orinoco**, the 60% bar, is a blend of Venezuela and Colombia with some Ghana; **Pariguan** is a 69% from

NAME OF THE BAR *La Maison du Chocolat Pariguan Chocolat Noir 69%*

COCOA SOLIDS, BLEND OR ORIGIN *69%, Venezuela, from Porcelana beans from Pedregal*

INGREDIENTS *Cocoa paste, brown sugar, cocoa butter, emulsifier: soy lecithin, natural extract: vanilla*

WEIGHT OF BAR *75g*

BAR MADE *Paris, France*

WEBSITE *www.lamaisonduchocolat.com*

AROMA *Red plum, red berry fruits, milky*

TASTE *Elegant and very long; the creamy mild melt builds to a rich mid-palate with a punch of acidity. The flavours begin to fade and then the acidity comes rolling back.*

PROFILE

Floral		Nutty	🌿
Fruity	🌿🌿🌿	Spicy	
Winey	🌿🌿🌿	Toasty	🌿
Honey	🌿🌿	Smoky	
Creamy	🌿🌿	Earthy	🌿

Venezuela (see profile above); and **Cuana**, a 74% blend from South and Central America and Africa. The flavoured bars are **Marao** 60% with almonds and **Talamanca** milk 37% with hazelnuts.

To be honest, one would not go to La Maison du Chocolat just for the chocolate bars. The shops are a temple to truffles, pralines, ganaches and other chocolate temptations.

Laurent Gerbaud

Brussels is a paradise for chocolate lovers: a city overrun by chocolate shops full of buttery, creamy concoctions and golden packaging. Chocolatier Laurent Gerbaud stands out from the crowd. He has lived in China, and this shows in many details of his approach. It starts with the design of his packaging.

BAIES ROUGES DE PERSE
Persian Cranberries
Chocolat Noir 70% – 65 g ℮ – 2.29 oz

The flavourings of his bars show a zenlike restraint, from the **Baies Rouges de Perse** (Persian cranberries, featured in the profile on the facing page) to the **Mendiants** 70% which is decorated on the back with grilled and salted nuts and dried fruits – grilled, salted and sugary, with a dart of acidity, set against the supple darkness of the chocolate, it is a subtle, elegant treat. A little more salty is the **Pistaches d'Evoïa** – the grilled and salted pistachios are a perfect match for the greater milkiness of the 50% bar. Gerbaud likes to press fruits and nuts onto the back of bar rather than mix them in with the chocolate. This method always looks good but risks tasting uneven. Gerbaud is one of the few who makes it work.

The oriental influences are highlighted in his 'travel book' range of flavours: **Yuzu** (Japanese citrus), **Calabrian Bergamot**, **Spirit of Christmas** and **Sweet Chili**. Each 50g bar comes in a discreet white folded wallet and the chocolate mould is imprinted with the pattern of a Chinese seal, which Gerbaud uses as a logo. The characters spell the word 'chocolat' (*tchio-ke-li*) plus his initials, L G. The bergamot, a bitter-tasting citrus fruit, is candied, and the lime/bitter orange flavour subtly blossoms on the tongue in a balance of fine fruit pieces and smooth chocolate.

NAME OF THE BAR *Laurent Gerbaud Baies Rouges de Perse 70%*
COCOA SOLIDS, BLEND OR ORIGIN *70%, Ecuador and the Sambirano Valley,*
Madagascar
INGREDIENTS *Dark chocolate 70% cocoa minimum (cocoa paste, cocoa butter, cane sugar),*
dried cranberries (15%)
WEIGHT OF BAR *65g*
BAR MADE *Brussels, Belgium*
WEBSITE *www.chocolatsgerbaud.be*
AROMA *Dark, fine roast, red fruits*
TASTE *Smooth elegant melt. A complex, harmonious blend. The finish shows bitter notes*
which are eased by the chewy cranberries.

PROFILE

Floral			Nutty	
Fruity	🌶🌶🌶		Spicy	🌶
Winey	🌶🌶🌶		Toasty	🌶🌶
Honey	🌶		Smoky	🌶
Creamy	🌶🌶		Earthy	🌶

Gerbaud is a relatively rare chocolatier who acknowledges the source of his chocolate or couverture. Domori (see page 114) in Italy is his supplier, and they make him an exclusive blend of Madagascar Trinitario beans from the Sambirano Valley 'for richness and intensity' and Ecuadorian Nacional beans 'for exceptional length'. His dark bars are made without soya lecithin to ensure that 'the blend is as close as possible to the original chocolate recipe'. Gerbaud stresses 'our chocolates are free of lots of things: gluten, alcohol, preservatives, additives and artificial flavourings.'

Lindt & Sprüngli

Is it Lindt or is it Sprüngli? It is both, although there is a strong argument for saying the company that produces everything from bars to life-size gold-foiled Easter bunnies should really be known as Sprüngli. The Sprüngli history begins in Zurich in 1845, when a patissier decided to make the chocolate bars that were becoming so fashionable in Italy. These Sprüngli bars were a success, and the business grew. In 1892 the company was divided between two sons, one taking over the shops, the other the chocolate factory. In 1899, the chocolatier purchased the business and business secrets of Rodolphe Lindt, who had invented the conch and so created a fine, melting chocolate or *chocolat fondant*, a term still used today.

This company then became Lindt & Sprüngli. In the early 20th century there was a serious falling-out with the Lindts. After an expensive battle a rival business, set up by the Lindts, was 'liquidated', as the company history puts it. Since then, Lindt & Sprüngli has grown into a global business, and along the way has purchased other well-known chocolate businesses, including Turin's Caffarel in 1997 and San Francisco's Ghirardelli in 1998.

I have a special affection for Lindt as it was my introduction to 'grown-up' chocolate. My father liked the slim tablets of dark chocolate, wrapped in thin silver foil and packed in a pink card case. With those bars I first discovered the theatre of good packaging and

NAME OF THE BAR *Lindt Excellence Intense Dark 70%*

COCOA SOLIDS, BLEND OR ORIGIN *70%*

INGREDIENTS *Cocoa mass, sugar, cocoa butter, natural Bourbon vanilla beans*

WEIGHT OF BAR *100g*

BAR MADE *'Six production sites in Europe, two in the USA'*

WEBSITE *www.lindt.com; www.lindtexcellence.com*

AROMA *Floral and creamy, suggesting a sweeter bar*

TASTE *A crowd pleaser: the flavours develop slowly. Darts of grapefruit pierce the deep chocolate core. The mid-palate is broad and creamy with a long slow melt with a brisk citrus finish. A successful blend, if just a little anonymous.*

PROFILE

Floral	🍃		Nutty	
Fruity	🍃🍃🍃		Spicy	
Winey	🍃🍃		Toasty	🍃
Honey	🍃🍃		Smoky	
Creamy	🍃🍃		Earthy	🍃

the pleasure of unwrapping. I also discovered that chocolate can disappoint, because despite the allure of the packaging I did not like the bitter flavour.

Today Lindt makes a 99% bar, which I definitely would have disliked as a child. It is part of the 'Excellence' range, launched in 1989, which marked the beginning of the trend for bars. There is an impressive series of plain bars in the range, from milk through to 99%, with a fine snap. Lindt's 'Excellence' bars are among the most widely available internationally and so for many people they represent the standard for dark chocolate.

The flavoured bars are becoming ever more adventurous and now include **Chilli** as well as the more traditional **Orange**. The latest entrant to the range is **Sea Salt**, which definitely proves that sea salt has joined the mainstream as a successful partner with dark chocolate.

Madécasse

The fourth largest island in the world, Madagascar is proving a real draw for the chocolate world. The Sambirano Valley on the north-west tip of the island produces a chocolate that has an appealing warmth and gentleness. The place itself has the same allure, especially because of its isolation. By nature of Madagascar's status as the tenth poorest country in the world, agriculture on the island is organic, and so the environment for cacao is healthy.

This statistic comes from Madécasse's founders, Brett Beach and Tim McCollum, both of whom worked on the island with the Peace Corps. Beach stayed on, working for USAID, before returning to the United States to set up a chocolate company with McCollum in 2006. They chose the name, Madécasse, pronounced 'Mad-day-cass', because it is a name that was used for the island in the 16th and 17th centuries. Their project is simple if not completely straightforward. The beans are grown and fermented in the Sambirano Valley, and then made into finished chocolate bars in the highlands region of Madagascar. The business also grows and makes products from vanilla. The growers, therefore, are following a different model from the usual cacao trade. By adding value themselves, Beach and McCollum estimate, they are getting a fourfold increase in income on what they would have had by selling the beans on to a multinational company.

The company makes a range of bars – at 63%, 65%, 70% and 75%. Is it really possible to distinguish between such narrow bands of difference? In the case of Madécasse most definitely. The range of styles is striking. The 63% has lively

NAME OF THE BAR *Madécasse 70%*

COCOA SOLIDS, BLEND OR ORIGIN *70%, Sambirano Valley, Madagascar*

INGREDIENTS *Cocoa beans, sugar, cocoa butter, soy lecithin, natural vanilla*

WEIGHT OF BAR *75g*

BAR MADE *Madagascar*

WEBSITE *www.madecasse.com*

AROMA *Cocoa, red fruits, honey*

TASTE *The chocolate starts gently, full of mild, milky chocolate; then the red fruits promised in the aroma arrive to fill out the mid-palate. Finally, there is a bite of earthy woody notes as a reminder that cacao is a bean that has to be tamed.*

PROFILE

Floral	🍪		Nutty	🍪
Fruity	🍪🍪🍪		Spicy	🍪
Winey	🍪🍪		Toasty	🍪🍪
Honey	🍪		Smoky	🍪🍪
Creamy	🍪		Earthy	🍪🍪🍪

aromas of red fruits and honey, and in the mouth melts in a rather fudgy fashion into a satisfying blend of molasses and cream to create a rich, soothing sensation. There is just a hint of bitterness on the finish to prove that nothing is quite as perfect as it seems. The 67% has a less appealing balsamic and herbal aroma, and a powerful citrus aspect that dominates. The 70% is reviewed above. The 75% is surprisingly smooth for a 75% bar – nothing stands out on the palate, although it lasts well with a dominant sensation of chocolate. A bar at 80% and one with sea salt and nibs are recent introductions to the range.

Malmö Chokladfabrik

Swedish chocolate for many outside Sweden means Daim bars or the Marabou brand. For Swedes there is also a childhood memory of homemade *chokladbollar* (chocolate balls). However, there is now a flourishing chocolate renaissance in Sweden.

One of the names that predates the new enthusiasm for chocolate is Malmö Chokladfabrik, based in southern Sweden. Founded, as the branding of the bars suggests, in 1888, it has recently been enlivened by new owners. The company runs a small chocolate museum, covering the history of the company and of chocolate. They say that Malmö is 'the only Swedish quality chocolate produced all the way from cocoa beans'. (Åkesson's, see page 64, are Swedish but do not make their own chocolate.)

Malmö emphasise that they do not use soya lecithin or vanilla in their plain bars. The Fairtrade 70% has powerful aromas of red fruits and perhaps even Swedish lingonberries, and a fresh hit of sharp red fruits. The texture is grainy, though the melt is long, and the flavour develops slowly into a smoky earthiness with just a note of tannin.

The flavoured bars are less successful. The **Peppermint** 65% has a powerful minty note too reminiscent of the dentist to charm a chocolate eater. The **Lime** 70% has an uncanny note of shower gel. The 'Bits n' Pieces' range has **Cardamom**

NAME OF THE BAR *Malmö Chokladfabrik 1888 Master Blend*
COCOA SOLIDS, BLEND OR ORIGIN *70%*
INGREDIENTS *Cocoa mass, cane sugar, cocoa butter, 'free from foreign fats, soy lecithin and vanilla'*
WEIGHT OF BAR *80g*
BAR MADE *Malmö, Sweden*
WEBSITE *www.malmochokladfabrik.se*
AROMA *Creamy, floral, lightly roasted*
TASTE *Bold, dark and fruity: opens up with a dark, sludgy, roasted profile, with toasty notes, lightened by green apples and strawberries which come through strongly. The flavours linger. A grainy smokiness gives a rough elegance. Finishes with a bite of liquorice.*

PROFILE

Floral	🌶🌶		Nutty	🌶
Fruity	🌶🌶🌶		Spicy	🌶
Winey	🌶🌶🌶		Toasty	🌶🌶
Honey	🌶		Smoky	🌶🌶
Creamy	🌶🌶		Earthy	🌶🌶

65% – a keynote Swedish flavour. Another favourite Swedish flavour is **Lingonberry**, which is handled with pleasing subtlety. The **Sea Salt** 65% is interesting, though in general sea salt works better with a milkier bar.

Malmö Chokladfabrik has relaunched itself for the 21st century, while still remaining true to its traditions. There are other new Swedish chocolatiers appearing. Some of them are creating bonbons with exceptional technical beauty, others are taking inspiration from Sweden's fruit and spices. Names to look out for include Mälarchocolaterie (*ww.mcl.se*), Robert E's Choklad (*www.robertes-choklad.com*), Jan Hedh & Maria Escalante (*www.escalante.se*), also in Malmö, and Emanuel Andrén (*www.emanuelandren.com*).

Mast Brothers Brooklyn

Just when it seems that every artisan niche in the chocolate world has been filled, a new business comes along. Welcome to the Mast Brothers, who unlike the usual marketing hype are really brothers and are really called Mast. Their particular niche is that they are (for the time being at least) New York City's only bean-to-bar maker.

Rick's culinary career has seen him in the kitchens of such fashionable names as the Gramercy Tavern and Soho House, as well as with chocolatier Jacques Torres. When not crafting chocolate, he plays the banjo and piano: he is a classicaly trained musician. Michael was once upon a time in finance for independent films, which must surely explain the Gold Rush era silent movie feel of the website.

Mast Brothers' trade mark, American Craft Chocolate, is not just a trivial piece of sloganising. Their whole approach to manufacture and to marketing is that of craftsmen. It is symbolised by the wrappers for their bars, which are made from handmade papers of the sort favoured by bookbinders – and even, perish the thought, by handmade soaps. It has to be said, the handwork means these smart, chic bars are not cheap.

The brothers source their cacao beans from small growers in Venezuela, Madagascar and the Dominican Republic. The 72% **Madagascar** is their one plain bar at present; the flavoured bars are all dark and include **Fleur de Sel**, **Almonds and Sea Salt** and **Cocoa Nibs**, in addition to seasonal bars such as **Cranberry**.

NAME OF THE BAR *Mast Brothers Dark Chocolate 72% Madagascar*
COCOA SOLIDS, BLEND OR ORIGIN *72%, Madagascar, organic cacao*
INGREDIENTS *Cacao, cane sugar, 'vegan product'; 'roasted in small batches. Hand cracked. Refined using granite stone and aged'*
WEIGHT OF BAR *2.5oz*
BAR MADE *Brooklyn, New York, USA*
WEBSITE *www.mastbrotherschocolate.com*
AROMA *Deep, creamy, mocha character*

TASTE *The bar looks anonymous, with no branding and just a few scuffed edges. The flavour is anything but anonymous. The first blast is of grapefruit, then comes the grip of dry tannin. This is followed quickly by the richness of the cacao, blended with raspberries. The flavours stay at a peak for a long time, and then slowly fade in a blend of citrus and toast. Very persistent. A real character that holds the attention.*

PROFILE

Floral		Nutty	
Fruity	❦❦❦	Spicy	
Winey	❦❦❦	Toasty	❦❦
Honey	❦	Smoky	❦❦
Creamy		Earthy	❦❦❦

Above: Rick (left) and Michael Mast: from bean to bar in Brooklyn.

Melt

'Motherhood and apple pie' is a catchphrase that gives an indisputably warm feeling. In Louise Nason's case it should perhaps be 'motherhood and choco-late'. Melt is a chocolate boutique that definitely appears to welcome mums and children: mums, who can drop in once the chil-dren are at school; children at the end of the school day, keen for the treat of a chocolate lollipop and a

chance to watch the in-house chocolatier at work. Nason, a mother of four, understands those after-school munchy moments.

Nason and her husband started the business in 2006 in one of London's smart 'villages', Notting Hill. The shop is a bright, airy modern space, all white surfaces and glass. Customers can create their own boxed selections of her chocolates, selecting with wooden tongs from tempting open trays in the shop. (For fun, there is a truncated version on the website.)

The chocolatier working at the back of the shop is a real draw. First in the post was Damian Allsop, whose speciality is water-based ganaches (that is, with no dairy ingredients). Today Chikako (Chika) Watanabe is the in-house choco-latier. Previously she worked in a bank in Tokyo, but in 2001 came to Europe to study chocolate and pastry. In addition to her truffles and bonbons, you can also buy boxes of chocolates commissioned by well-known chefs and restau-rants including The River Café (Amedei '9' truffles), Sophie Conran (Earl Grey tea ganache, with ginger and cranberry), and Mark Hix (milk chocolate-coated fudge with Cornish sea salt, and a dark chocolate ganache with Somerset Cider Apple Brandy).

NAME OF THE BAR *Melt Bar 1*
COCOA SOLIDS, BLEND OR ORIGIN *66%, Criollo and Trinitario, 'a unique blend*
of chocolate from Venezuela, Madagascar and Ecuador'
INGREDIENTS *Cocoa solids, sugar, cocoa butter, vanilla, soya lecithin*
WEIGHT OF BAR *90g*
BAR MADE *London, England*
WEBSITE *www.meltchocolates.com*
AROMA *Darkly chocolatey, with creamy nutty highlights*
TASTE *The thick squares need a firm bite and are slow to melt; they start bitter with citrus and roasted coffee notes; smoothed over by the rich, fudgy mid-palate. A crunch of acidity shows through on the palate. Long finish, with a brisk grip of tannin.*

PROFILE

Floral		Nutty	
Fruity	🍫🍫	Spicy	🍫
Winey		Toasty	🍫🍫
Honey	🍫	Smoky	🍫🍫
Creamy	🍫	Earthy	🍫🍫

One of Melt's original suppliers of couverture was the Colombian Chocolate Santander (see page 98). They have started to work with The Grenada Chocolate Company (see page 130) and Amano (see page 68) as well.

Melt's own bars have grown to a rainbow of 16, each packed in a coloured card sleeve. In addition to the plain dark bars, there are a number of quirkier styles: **Melt Bar 4** is white chocolate with tangerine zest, grapefruit oil, cocoa nibs and rosemary; **Popcorn** is a milk chocolate bar with caramelised popcorn; and **Melt Strip Bar** is milk chocolate with a strip of sesame seeds. These are square, solid, chunky 90g bars: while they may not all succeed completely, there is an enticing range of flavours.

Michael Mischer

Dark Chocolate - 72% Cacao
Single Origin - Criollo

The San Francisco Bay area is alive with chocolatiers. Some 150 years ago Ghirardelli and Guittard (see page 134) started up their chocolate businesses and the city has not looked back since. The renaissance really began with John Scharffenberger and Robert Steinberg who founded Scharffen Berger (see page 200) in 1996, and Michael Recchiuti whose elegant confections include every kind of fine chocolate treat. Today there are several West Coast chocolate artisans, ranging from Santa Cruz south of San Francisco (see Richard Donnelly page 192) north to Ashland in southern Oregon (see Dagoba page 106) and Seattle (see Theo page 212).

Michael Mischer is a producer who straddles the worlds of both filled chocolates and bars. His background is European: born in Germany, he trained as a patissier. However, onto that formal education in traditional techniques and flavours was overlaid a sunny California sensibility when he moved there in 1984.

The chocolate business began with filled chocolates, some classic (*gianduja*, marzipan), some less so (tamarind, root beer). The flavoured bars have some of the same radical appeal. He flavours these riotous hunks of chocolate by pressing the ingredient(s) into the back of the bar. The chocolate he uses is from Trinitario or Criollo beans, and many of his flavoured bars are nearly all available in a choice of 38%, 65% and 72% cocoa solids. There are bars sprinkled with hazelnuts for the traditionally inclined; **Cayenne-spiced Mango**, or **Orange & Togarashi** (Japanese 7-spice mix), or **Blueberry & Dragon Fruit**

NAME OF THE BAR *Michael Mischer Dark Chocolate 72% Single Origin Criollo*
COCOA SOLIDS, BLEND OR ORIGIN *72%, Ecuador*
INGREDIENTS *Cocoa mass, sugar, cocoa butter, vanilla*
WEIGHT OF BAR *3.2oz*
BAR MADE *Oakland, California, USA*
WEBSITE *www.michaelmischerchocolates.com*
AROMA *Chocolatey with red fruits*
TASTE *Well-moulded bar that breaks with a clean snap. The flavours are equally clean and pure, making a dark bar that is just the right side of bitter, with mild milky undertones. Very well balanced, with a long finish that suggests harsh tannin but escapes it. Elegant.*

PROFILE

Floral		Nutty	🌸🌸
Fruity	🌸	Spicy	🌸
Winey	🌸	Toasty	🌸🌸
Honey	🌸🌸	Smoky	
Creamy	🌸🌸	Earthy	🌸

for the fruit-minded; and my favourite, **Toffee and Murray River Salt**. This is an entirely over-the-top mix of sweet toffee, dark chocolate and smoky Australian salt flakes that demands an espresso coffee on the side. It is very easy to squish dried fruits into the back of a bar – only a few producers make it work. Mischer, with his blend of traditional and modern, is getting it just about right.

Michel Cluizel

Cluizel is one of the bar producers who gets chocolate lovers talking: put together a group of keen followers of chocolate bars and each will have an opinion and a favourite from the Cluizel range. My real favourites are the **Grué** 60%, the wondrously textured bar with nibs, and the Papua New Guinea **Maralumi** plantation milk 47%. This is probably my all-time favourite chocolate bar, with a blend of milkiness, a crunch of red fruits and a caramel finish with a pinch of salt. Others prefer to argue between the different plantation 'crus' or origins. Whatever your favourite, the important thing is that Cluizel has a remarkably high rate of success, so it is always worth trying a new bar.

Michel Cluizel joined his parents' patisserie in Normandy in 1948 and today his children also work in the business. Cluizel is one of France's rare producers working with beans he has sourced direct from the plantations, making bars and chocolates as well as couvertures for the industry. He has two shops, one in Paris and one in New York.

Cluizel is a good place to start on a journey into the flavours of chocolate, as he does not add soya lecithin, and like Domori (see page 114), has excellent tasting notes on the back of the packet. **Concepcion** 66%, from the Barlovento valley of Venezuela, does indeed let you 'gradually discover hints of vanilla, honey spice cake and caramel in a ... remarkable length with accents of mixed dried and black fruits'. I like the way the notes suggest in a rather sensual way that the chocolate 'lets you' discover it, that it is in charge. **Villa Gracinda** 67% is a fascinating introduction to São Tomé, as so much of the

NAME OF THE BAR *Michel Cluizel Noir de Cacao 72%*
COCOA SOLIDS, BLEND OR ORIGIN *72%, 'composed of cacaos from South America, Africa and Java'*
INGREDIENTS *Cacaos, cane sugar, cacao butter, Bourbon vanilla pod*
WEIGHT OF BAR *100g*
BAR MADE *Normandy, France*
WEBSITE *www.cluizel.com*
AROMA *Boldly earthy, with minty notes*
TASTE *Very well presented bar with a brisk snap. The inital impression is of molasses, then coconut; the mid-palate is surprisingly creamy and honeyed for a 72% bar. The finish is very slow, with a slight grain of tannin building. The richness of the chocolate is balanaced by a fine acidity. A fine blend, though some Cluizel fans may prefer his specialist 'crus' or flavoured bars.*

PROFILE

Floral		Nutty	🌶🌶
Fruity	🌶	Spicy	🌶🌶
Winey		Toasty	🌶
Honey	🌶🌶🌶	Smoky	🌶
Creamy	🌶🌶🌶	Earthy	🌶

chocolate from that island is quite tough to like. This has Cluizel's characteristic excellent finish, snap and melt. Beyond that there are challenging notes – burnt rubber, tobacco, a scent of gang warfare with screeching bikes on hot tarmac. Yet it finishes smoothly in the warm Cluizel blanket. **Los Anconès**, 67% from Santo Domingo, has many fans: again, the Cluizel finish charms, while the chocolate produces astonishing olive notes.

Cluizel welcomes visitors to its museum, or Chocolatrium, in Normandy, with a good blend of education and indulgence.

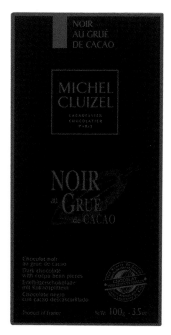

Montezuma's

Montezuma's is an English company that is all about chocolate from organically grown ingredients, fairly traded, with a selection that is suitable for vegans (that is, free from animal products). The owners, Helen and Simon Pattinson, gave up their careers as lawyers to become, as they put it, 'chocolate entrepreneurs'. They started in the year 2000, and have built a loyal following of consumers who appreciate their ethical outlook.

Their style is bold and humorous. Their flavours illustrate the tastes of their more adventurous, younger consumers. There is a box of highly spiced truffles: wasabi, ginger, chilli, salt and curry spice. 'Montezuma's Revenge' encapsulates their approach: it is a dark chocolate truffle with lime, chilli and tequila. There is a **Chilli & Lime** bar, originally invented for a local chilli festival. Other flavours include **Peppermint & Vanilla**, **Orange & Geranium**, **Butterscotch** and **Nutmeg**. Organic cacao comes mainly from the Dominican Republic, and Montezuma's has **Dark**, **Milk** and **White** bars from this origin. It also offers other origin bars, from Ecuador, Venezuela, Peru and Papua New Guinea.

The bars are packed in cardboard boxes full of information about the company and its ethical standpoint. The bars do not look entirely promising, with a few air holes, and some crumbling round the edges. However, the **Chilli & Lime**, at 34% cocoa solids, although it does not have a clean snap, melts well, and the chilli is well controlled, building gently on the back palate. The lime is a sensible addition, just as it is in guacamole, lifting the richness of the chocolate and cooling the burn.

NAME OF THE BAR *Dark Chocolate Organic 70% Peru*
COCOA SOLIDS, BLEND OR ORIGIN *70% Peru*
INGREDIENTS *Organic cocoa solids, organic sugar*
WEIGHT OF BAR *100g*
BAR MADE *Chichester, West Sussex, England*
WEBSITE *www.montezumas.co.uk*
AROMA *Earthy, leafy*
TASTE *A mild, chocolatey bar with coconut and vanilla notes; it finishes with a firm, tannic bite with a drying note.*

PROFILE

Floral		Nutty	🌿🌿
Fruity	🌿	Spicy	🌿🌿
Winey		Toasty	🌿🌿
Honey	🌿🌿	Smoky	🌿🌿
Creamy	🌿	Earthy	🌿🌿

The chocolate is disappointingly milky, verging on the fudgy, but this is clearly the balance that their customers enjoy.

Would Montezuma (or Motecuhzoma Xocoyotzin, to give him his full name), the last Aztec king, after whom the brand is named, recognise his legacy? Surely not, for cacao has come a long way since the Aztecs in the early 16th century. It is surprising, though, that it took a small organic chocolate manufacturer in southern England to build a brand out of the most famous name in the history of chocolate.

Right: Montezuma, the last Aztec king.

NewTree

Founded in Belgium in 2001, by a choco-late-loving biochemist, NewTree's mission is apparently to 'bring new life to the great tradition of Belgian chocolate'. It is a worthy ambition, but also a huge one, to attempt to resuscitate a rotund, buttery, creamy creation and set it on a slim new path. Certainly these self-styled 'natural born chocolates' are very different in flavour from the old-school Belgian luxury brigade, and there is not a drop of white chocolate in sight.

From the beginning NewTree was aligning itself with New Age philosophies. The first collection of bars included one bar with blackcurrant and another with lavender, for their antioxidant and tranquility-inducing properties respectively. The range has grown, and there is now a selection of entic-ingly labelled bars which are all to do with pleasure, though little perhaps to do with chocolate: **Pleasure**, **Vigor**, **Renew**, **Refresh**, **Forgiveness** (with lemon and 'a natural cactus extract rich in fiber'), **Sexy** (with ginger and guarana), and **Blush** (with cherry, 'one 2.8oz bar provides more antioxidants than two glasses of red wine'). The business is certainly in tune with today's health interests, but it will need to continue to support its work with independent research.

In 2008, NewTree boasted a chocolate first by producing a bar with Omega 3 fatty acids, basically by including flax seeds. These slippery seeds bear a startling resemblance to bird food; while chocolate makes them interesting, it surely spoils a good chocolate.

NAME OF THE BAR *NewTree Noir Cacao 73% Pleasure*
COCOA SOLIDS, BLEND OR ORIGIN *73%*
INGREDIENTS *Cocoa mass, sugar, pure cocoa butter, skimmed powdered cocoa,*
emulsifier: soy lecithin
WEIGHT OF BAR *80g*
BAR MADE *Belgium*
WEBSITE *www.newtree.com*
AROMA *Herbal, leafy, minty, earthy*
TASTE *A good snap and sheen. An exceptionally mild profile: the flavours are creamy and milky, and delicately chocolatey, with liquorice and roasted coffee. Finish is light and grainy.*

PROFILE

Floral		Nutty	🌿🌿
Fruity		Spicy	🌿🌿
Winey		Toasty	🌿
Honey	🌿	Smoky	
Creamy	🌿	Earthy	🌿🌿

NewTree is very clear that it does not claim to process beans: 'We source the chocolate, not the beans', adding, 'we are sensitive to the labour issues around cacao farming and do not support any company along the supply chain involved with exploitative labour practices.'

Oberweis

In 1964 Nelson Mandela was condemned to life imprisonment; the United States had its first experience of Beatlemania, as screaming fans of the UK pop group, the Beatles, stormed JFK airport; Tanganyika and Zanzibar merged to form Tanzania; and Martin Luther King Jr received the Nobel Peace Prize.

Meanwhile in Luxembourg Pit Oberweis and his wife Monique were busy establishing a patisserie business – there is a wonderful period photo on the website of Monique with a chic beehive hairdo working in their first shop. With their commitment to quality they became authorised suppliers to the Court, or 'Fournisseur de la Cour', of the Grand Duchy of Luxembourg. Pit developed a reputation as a classical patissier, and also as a teacher and trainer in the profession, and a judge at the leading competitions. Pit and Monique's sons, Tom and Jeff, both joined the business, and they have since been joined by their wives, Nicole and Léa.

Visiting any of their premises today, from the 350-seat restaurant at the Cloche d'Or to the outlet at the Central Station, it is difficult not to be distracted by the savoury bites and foods to take away, or by the fashionable repertoire of macaroons, tarts and ice creams. Their understanding of flavour and texture transfers itself perfectly to their bars.

NAME OF THE BAR *Oberweis 70% cacao Venezuela*
COCOA SOLIDS, BLEND OR ORIGIN *70% Venezuela Criollo*
INGREDIENTS *Cocoa butter, sugar, cocoa mass, emulsifier: soya lecithin*
WEIGHT OF BAR *100g*
BAR MADE *Luxembourg*
WEBSITE *www.oberweis.lu*
AROMA *Deep, rich aromas of tobacco, earth and spices, promising powerful flavours*
TASTE *The entry is smooth, cool and almost minty, the melt is gradual, only slowly releasing flavours of coconut cream and hazelnuts in their skins, as the graininess develops in the mouth; though there is no vanilla listed, the taste of vanilla persists, followed by a warm, intensely chocolatey finish and a light, dry grip.*

PROFILE

Floral	🌱	Nutty	🌱
Fruity	🌱	Spicy	🌱
Winey		Toasty	
Honey	🌱🌱	Smoky	🌱
Creamy	🌱🌱🌱	Earthy	🌱

Their milk chocolate (37%) with **Noix de cajou caramelisées à la fleur de sel** (cashew nuts and sea salt) is an adventure in a chocolate world where almonds and hazelnuts are more common. Cashews are rich, but are well balanced by crunchy caramel and sea salt. The 61% **Citron & Genièvre** (lemon and juniper) is an elegant riot, a gin-drinker's delight. Subtly handled, there is the slightest suggestion of citrus while the juniper appears first as a grainy texture and then the merest hint of spice.

The plain bars are weighty, 100g blocks, simply wrapped, with a good, brisk snap. The 40% **Côte d'Ivoire** has a hollow core, but a warm, mocha milkiness. The 64% **Madagascar** is an appealing purple/mahogany colour, and reveals the fruity profile of the island's cacao. The initial promise is of red fruits, which is rounded by a boom of chocolate, and lifted by darts of citrus.

Original Beans

Philipp Kauffmann, one of the founders of Original Beans, was clearly destined for the business. Back in 1791 one of his ancestors wrote a book on sustainable forest management. When Kauffmann eventually decided to continue the family passion and create 'a company that replenishes the planet', he chose the humble bean because 'cacao can do that with charisma'. With his partners, Rodney Nikkels and Lesal Ruskey (with backgrounds in agriculture and development), he has created a business that is definitely of the third millennium, both stylish and seriously committed to sustainability.

The elegantly packed bars have short, clever tasting notes, and each bar carries a code so you can link to a Google map of its origin. For every bar purchased, a tree will be planted, either cacao trees, or others that add to the diversity of the region. This is not just a gimmick – it is an educational device. This is cacao with a real sense of origin and the website includes photos of Original Beans' work. In the Democratic Republic of the Congo, in particular, the trio have been active in encouraging planting in deforested zones. In Bolivia, they have gone to the Beni region of the Amazon, and in Ecuador to the Esmeraldas region close to Colombia.

Original Beans also makes a feature of its experimentation with conching, and the length of time is printed on the label. The **Esmeraldas Milk with Fleur de Sel** 42% cacao: 50-hour conch, from Ecuador, has a delectable smoothness. It also has a pinch of sea salt; so slight it is hard to tell, but in a way that lifts the creaminess. The Bolivian **Beni Wild Harvest** 68%, has been conched for 60 hours. The 70% **Cru Virunga**, from

NAME OF THE BAR *Original Beans Cru Virunga, D.R. Congo, 70% cacao, 20-hour conch*

COCOA SOLIDS, BLEND OR ORIGIN *70%; 'the first ever single-source chocolate from the Congo: the heart of Africa'*

INGREDIENTS *'Directly traded cacao beans, sugar, cacao butter … that's it'*

WEIGHT OF BAR *100g*

BAR MADE *Switzerland*

WEBSITE *www.originalbeans.com*

AROMA *Earthy, liquorice, berry fruits, coffee, balsamic, a little wild*

TASTE *A good snap. By contrast with the aromas, the flavours build slowly. A drift of smoke appears, covered by mouthwatering kumquat with orange peel, a little red berry, nutmeg and delicately floral notes and a milky finish. A fine grainy texture builds, giving a juicy grip. Very well-balanced. The lingering sweetness makes it a good choice for experimenters with dark bars.*

PROFILE

Floral	🌿	Nutty	🌿🌿
Fruity	🌿🌿	Spicy	🌿
Winey	🌿	Toasty	🌿
Honey	🌿🌿	Smoky	🌿
Creamy	🌿🌿	Earthy	🌿

the D. R. Congo, has had just 20 hours conching. All of them are technically beautifully presented, marked into 12 'finger' pieces with a good sheen, a great example of the transformation of the beans by Felchlin (see pages 228–9). They are, indeed, originals.

Pacari

Pacari – which means 'nature' in Quechua, an indigenous language of Ecuador – caters for every consumer need: '100% Arriba Nacional; Certified Organic; Single-Origin; Bean to Bar in Ecuador; Kosher; Dairy Free; Gluten Free; Rich in Antioxidants'. The two most important words here are 'Ecuador' and 'Antioxidants'. Santiago Peralta and Carla Barboto have started up a chocolate business in Ecuador designed to support the growers and their families, preserve the local Arriba Nacional cacao, and create a sustainable business that makes and sells its own chocolate, rather than shipping the beans to a factory overseas. Some of their producers are Fairtrade certified; Peralta and Barboto say that they ensure that all their producers pay fair wages and follow strict guidelines on working conditions.

The antioxidants are what has captured the attention of wholefood retailers. With 'Raw' written in bright green on the box, it is an immediate draw to consumers living in societies where foodstuffs are highly processed. Pacari state that 'in our 100% raw chocolate, all of the cacao ingredients are minimally processed and kept at low temperatures to maintain the antioxidants and complex flavour profile of our carefully selected cacao'. Certainly, at low temperatures, the cacao will retain many beneficial antioxidants. The flavour claims are more difficult, as with well-handled heat the cacao releases its complex flavours; keeping temperatures low is not necessarily a good thing. It should be noted that this is not strictly raw, as there has been an element of processing, and that Pacari have chosen to add lecithin to aid the processing.

NAME OF THE BAR *Pacari Ecuadorian Organic Raw Chocolate 70% Cacao*
COCOA SOLIDS, BLEND OR ORIGIN *70%; 'the first single origin chocolate made entirely in Ecuador'*
INGREDIENTS *Cacao beans, evaporated cane juice, cacao butter, sunflower lecithin*
WEIGHT OF BAR *50g*
BAR MADE *Quito, Ecuador*
WEBSITE *www.pacarichocolate.com*
AROMA *Earthy, balsamic, green leaves, citric*
TASTE *The texture arrives before the flavour: rich and crumbly. There follows a burst of citrus acidity, with some floral aspects, bright darts of redcurrant juice making for a vibrant mid-palate, developing a chalky texture. Finish is mouthwatering with a surprisingly sweet lift. Powerful and persistent.*

PROFILE

Floral		Nutty	✿
Fruity	✿✿✿	Spicy	✿✿
Winey	✿✿✿	Toasty	
Honey	✿	Smoky	
Creamy	✿	Earthy	✿✿✿

The real question is what does it taste like? The taste profile here shows that Raw is a chocolate with plenty of character, even though the texture is grainy. There is a 72% bar, **Los Rios**, which makes a useful contrast. The beans are made into traditional chocolate. Undoubtedly it is more complex, and smoother. Yet Raw comes off well by comparison for the chocolate fan who loves a blast of wild aromas. There are other Ecuadorian origin dark bars: **Esmeraldas** 60% and **Manabi** 65%.

There are other Pacari products: the chocolate-coated, cocoa-dusted cacao beans are a curiosity; much more palatable are the chocolate-coated fruits, nuts, coffee beans and nibs.

Patric Chocolate

There is clearly something special about Missouri. The state is home to not one but two artisan bean-to-bar makers, in a nation where there are no more than a handful of genuine bean-to-bar producers. Shawn Askinosie (see page 78) is one Missouri resident, and Alan McClure of Patric Chocolate the other.

McClure set up his business in 2006. He had always been interested in food, taking his interest much further than most youngsters and making food from scratch. As a teenager he made his own croissants, chorizo, bread and peanut butter. He now makes his own cheese and cider and chocolate, saying he welcomes the challenge of anything that requires intellectual effort. Spending a year in France, in Lyon, was bound to be a defining time. There he encountered Valrhona (see page 216) and Bernachon (see page 82), the city's two most important chocolatiers. He returned home and, eventually, after much experimentation, started up his own business.

Why is it called Patric? Patric(k)is his middle name and he thought it looked better on the label than 'McClure chocolate'. His mission statement on his website could be a descriptor of the last two decades of fine chocolate: 'French tradition, Italian innovation, American revelation'. His packaging has a kind of classical elegance with an American spin.

NAME OF THE BAR *Patric Chocolate Micro-Batch Dark Chocolate 70%*
COCOA SOLIDS, BLEND OR ORIGIN *70%, Madagascar, Sambirano Valley*
INGREDIENTS *Cocoa beans, sugar*
WEIGHT OF BAR *50g*
BAR MADE *Colombia, Missouri, USA*
WEBSITE *www.patric-chocolate.com*
AROMA *Floral, red fruits, citrus*
TASTE *A fine snap and well-finished with 'P' lettering on the mould. The flavours appear quickly with dark chocolate, then citrus, red berries and red wine burst through. The mid-palate is bold and strong with a boom of high-roast cocoa and brisk acidity. The long finish rounds off with a lively bite of tannin.*

PROFILE

Floral	🍫		Nutty	
Fruity	🍫🍫🍫		Spicy	🍫
Winey	🍫🍫🍫		Toasty	🍫
Honey	🍫		Smoky	🍫🍫
Creamy	🍫		Earthy	🍫🍫

He credits the American artisan chocolatier Steve DeVries (*www.devrieschocolate.com*) for giving him good advice, but recognises that he has had to learn everything for himself, a comment with which the other newcomers to chocolate in these pages would agree.

McClure has clearly thought deeply about tasting chocolate as much as about making it. His range of Madagascar bars, all from the same origin, but with different cocoa solids – 67%, 70% (see profile above), 75% and 70% with nibs – show subtle nuances, as well as his commitment to a fine finish in the moulds themselves. He has now moved into sourcing beans from Venezuela, with a Rio Caribe bar from the Paria peninsula. He uses only his own cocoa butter, and no vanilla or artificial flavourings.

Paul A Young

I first met Paul Young on a daytime television show, where he was making a fabulous cake. He was an unforgettable presence, a contrasting mix of domestic baker and creative artist, with a ringing north of England accent in a studio full of Londoners. He was also enthusiastic.

Young remains enthusiastic, and proud of his Yorkshire heritage. He still bakes the occasional really impressive cake, but his fondness for chocolate led him to set up his own shop in London in 2006, and then another in 2007. He had previously worked as a pastry chef in several London restaurants, including some of top chef Marco Pierre White's establishments, and has consulted in pastry and desserts for a major retailer.

His shops are full of bars, and bags of chocolates. There is also pride of place for brownies, since Young has made a feature of these ultra-gooey bakes. He has a specialist line in 'love them or hate them' truffles, with such radical flavours as Stilton and Port, and Marmite (but thankfully not together). His book, *Adventures with Chocolate*, includes some highly original recipes. I have to say that I would not cook them all – 'Dark chocolate and chilli gnocchi', 'Santorini tomato ganache', to name just two – but recipes such as 'Muscovado chocolate cakes with cocoa nibs and

NAME OF THE BAR *Paul A Young 70% Dark Chocolate*
COCOA SOLIDS, BLEND OR ORIGIN *70%*
INGREDIENTS *Cocoa mass, cocoa butter, sugar, soya lecithin, natural vanilla extract*
WEIGHT OF BAR *50g*
BAR MADE *London, England*
WEBSITE *www.paulayoung.co.uk*
AROMA *Red fruits, floral, red wine, darkly chocolate.*
TASTE *Dark chocolate and red fruits collide as the flavours develop in the mouth. The melt is supple, and eases the palate to a smooth finish, with a vibrant freshness.*

PROFILE

Floral	🍫	Nutty	
Fruity	🍫🍫	Spicy	
Winey	🍫🍫	Toasty	🍫
Honey	🍫🍫	Smoky	🍫
Creamy	🍫	Earthy	

Mayan spiced syrup' show that he is a confident, creative chocolatier who understands texture and flavour.

The varied selection of bars includes flavoured bars such as **White Chocolate with Toasted Sesame Seeds and Sea Salt** and a 72% **Venezuela with Green Peppercorns**. Plain bars, from a range of origins including Venezuela, Madagascar and the Dominican Republic, are neatly moulded and wrapped in cellophane.

Left: An elegant shop for elegant chocolate. This is the Paul A Young shop in the City of London.

Pierre Marcolini

In Brussels, across the road from the elegant and traditional patissier–chocolatier Wittamer in the Place du Grand Sablon, there are not one but two Pierre Marcolini shops. While Wittamer looks to be focusing on producing a classic array of chocolates and savouries for his local customers, Pierre Marcolini gives the definite air of one who would conquer the world.

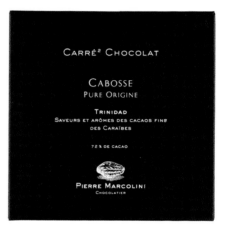

One of Marcolini's shops is a veritable temple to chocolate, looking like an upmarket Parisian jeweller. The chocolates are laid out as if they were diamonds. Go upstairs and one feels the frisson of being allowed apparently into the inner sanctum. The theatricality is enhanced by the signature black packaging with white highlights, and the excitement of the customers who have clearly come on a pilgrimage. They know that Marcolini is part of the contemporary vogue for celebrity chefs, and that he is keen to make a global impression with international stores in Paris, Kuwait and Japan.

NAME OF THE BAR *Pierre Marcolini Cabosse Pure Origine Trinidad 72%*
COCOA SOLIDS, BLEND OR ORIGIN *72%, Trinidad*
INGREDIENTS *Couverture chocolate minimum 72% cocoa (no vegetable fat), cane sugar,*
soy lecithin, vanilla pod from Tahiti, crushed cocoa beans
WEIGHT OF BAR *80g*
BAR MADE *Brussels, Belgium*
WEBSITE *www.marcolini.com*
AROMA *Floral, fruity, chocolatey*
TASTE *Clean snap, cleanly presented. The silky melt appears first, followed by notes of*
mocha coffee, and roasted beans. On the mid-palate there is a lively dart of redcurrant acidity
and a gently minty coolness. The flavours linger well, returning to the notes of coffee, with a
slight grip of earthy tannin.

PROFILE

Floral	🌼		Nutty	
Fruity	🌼🌼🌼		Spicy	
Winey	🌼🌼		Toasty	🌼🌼
Honey	🌼		Smoky	
Creamy	🌼		Earthy	🌼🌼

Pierre Marcolini's second shop in the square, 'La Manufacture', takes a slightly different approach. The style is post-modern, all glinting steel and glass. It is a welcome opportunity to see chocolatiers at work, however polished the presentation, in a city where the major brands are all about packaging.

Although Marcolini is Belgian, his filled chocolates are French in character. There is a wide range of bars – 80g squares marked into nine pieces with the letters of his name boldly engraved in sans serif capitals. They include single-estate productions from Java to Venezuela in the 'Grands Crus de Propriété' range at 72%, and 'Pures Origines', including a Venezuela–Ghana blend at 80% and a 50% Java milk. He also produces indulgent 'Plaisirs', a well-chosen selection including **Plaisir d'Enfance**, 72% Trinidad with Montélimar nougat, and **Plaisir Acidulé**, 72% Java with crystallised oranges and lemon drops. These are the bars of someone who clearly relishes the flavours of childhood.

Prestat

Prestat was founded in 1902, or possibly earlier (the archives have been lost), by a Frenchman called Antoine Dufour, who recognised the opportunity the wealthy city of London offered at that period. The team he recruited were all from continental Europe; clearly he could not trust British chefs with the pralines and truffles. It has long been a favourite with British royalty and the back of the bar states: 'As enjoyed by royalty and nobility, stars of the screen and stage and, even, by cardinals, bishops, abbots and nuns for over 100 years.'

Prestat was named after a relative, and being French the final 't' would certainly have been silent. Today the name has become firmly Anglo-Saxon with a ringing 'T' at the end. In the first part of the 20th century it had several stores in London, including one in the City – the role of feeding treats to financiers and bankers is one that Paul A Young (see page 182) took on at the beginning

of the 21st century with his tiny branch in the City of London. Eventually all that remained of the company was the shop in Mayfair, which became a destination for fans of this anglicised version of French chocolate. Prestat's truffles even featured in a novel, *My Uncle Oswald*, by Roald Dahl, better known for his children's book *Charlie and the Chocolate Factory*. In the novel, Prestat truffles doctored with a love potion are fed to the unsuspecting.

In recent years, Prestat has run through several owners, but has now settled down in Princes Arcade off London's Piccadilly under the ownership of two half-brothers. One, Bill Keeling, was formerly West Africa correspondent for the *Financial Times*, and has a keen interest in trading fairly with cacao farmers. With his half-brother, Nick Crean, he has repackaged the business, returning

NAME OF THE BAR *Prestat Organic Dark Chocolate Bar 63%*

COCOA SOLIDS, BLEND OR ORIGIN *63%; 'intensely rich dark chocolate made with our finest organic couvertures.'*

INGREDIENTS *Organic cocoa mass, organic cane sugar, organic cocoa butter, organic fat-reduced cocoa powder, emulsifier (soya lecithin)*

WEIGHT OF BAR *80g*

BAR MADE *London, England*

WEBSITE *www.prestat.co.uk*

AROMA *Initially earthy; then red fruits, followed by a suggestion of sweetness*

TASTE *A good snap to a bar that sits in the mid-range of flavours: creamy, honeyed, milky, relatively smooth and unchallenging. Just at the end there is the briefest of citrus lifts as the chocolate flavour comes through. The melt is just a little sludgy, and the finish falls away.*

PROFILE

Floral		Nutty	🍂🍂🍂
Fruity	🍂	Spicy	🍂
Winey		Toasty	🍂🍂
Honey	🍂🍂🍂	Smoky	🍂
Creamy	🍂🍂🍂	Earthy	🍂

it to the indulgence of times past but with a little new millennium colour. The bars are all organic: **Dark** 63%, **Dark with sweet orange** 63% (with a distinctively sludgy melt), **Milk** 35% and **Milk with roasted almonds**. They are neatly moulded with the company logo. The range is gradually expanding from its truffles, through bars to chocolate drops from named origins. Prestat's major innovation has been the creation of the antioxidant-rich Choxi brand (see page 100).

Rancho San Jacinto

Rancho San Jacinto started as a family business some 40 years ago with five cattle and 23 hectares (57 acres) of land close to the Gulf of Guayaquil in Ecuador. Today the Rancho has 1000 cattle and 500 hectares (1235 acres) of land, of which 115 hectares (285 acres) are devoted to cacao. In 1985 it worked with Don Homero Castro on the development of a new disease-resistant type of cacao known as CCN51. At the Rancho, as elsewhere in Ecuador, it is often known by the more attractive name of Don Homero, after its creator.

The genetics of Ecuadorian cacao is a topic of heated debate. In essence, much of Ecuador's cacao is a superior type of Forastero called Nacional. Some of this is known as Arriba or Arriba Nacional, as it originally came from the 'Arriba' or upper region. The arrival of CCN51 has muddied the waters, as the trees are inevitably crossing with each other, and also because many producers blend the two types of beans indiscriminately. At Rancho San Jacinto, they are explicit: on the back of the pack they state that both beans – Arriba Nacional and Don Homero – are used.

Initially the Rancho fermented, dried and roasted its beans, and then sold them on. Making bars is a more recent venture, following in the footsteps of other successful Ecuadorian businesses (see Kallari, page 142). The Rancho has Rainforest Alliance and BCS organic certification and the bars are attractively packaged and shrinkwrapped under the slogan 'Chocolate with Ecuadorian flavor'.

NAME OF THE BAR *Rancho San Jacinto 75%*
COCOA SOLIDS, BLEND OR ORIGIN *75%, Ecuador, 'the cacao used for our chocolate in its two varieties Arriba Nacional and Don Homero is processed … with Organic and Rainforest Alliance certifications'*
INGREDIENTS *Pure cocoa mass (roasted and ground cocoa beans), sugar. 'No vanilla or aroma added'*
WEIGHT OF BAR *100g*
BAR MADE *Guayaquil, Ecuador*
WEBSITE *www.rsanjacinto.com*
AROMA *Floral, nutty, creamy, fruity*
TASTE *Starts with an array of tropical fruits, along with lime juice and roasted coffee, with a hint of aniseed. Earthy notes develop in the mid-palate, building a mouthfilling richness with a grainy texture. There is a tannic finish, with light, dry grip.*

PROFILE

Floral		Nutty	⚘⚘
Fruity	⚘⚘	Spicy	
Winey	⚘	Toasty	⚘⚘
Honey	⚘	Smoky	⚘⚘
Creamy		Earthy	⚘⚘

Unwrapped, the bars have an unpromising appearance, slightly dusty and anonymous in their plain moulds. The snap is not entirely crisp, perhaps showing the typically higher fat content of the Don Homero bean. The 55% has a lively green apple and red berry flavour, with a note of dried fruit, coated with a chocolate milkiness, a little like a chocolate cake sandwiched with jam and cream. The 65% bar with chilli has a real bite, and would go well in a spicy *mole* sauce. The 75% is reviewed above. The 100% has dominant balsamic aromas and finishes surprisingly short. No vanilla or lecithin are used, and all the bars have a distinctive low acidity.

Red Star

It is safe to say that the owner-chocolatier of Red Star is the only Formula 1 racing car engineer featured in this book, and in the fine chocolate world. Duffy Sheardown's career goes back some way – he made the first F1 car for the late, great Brazilian driver Ayrton Senna, in 1984.

His engineering skills transfer readily to his new career as a chocolatier; he knows how to tinker successfully with machines. He bought his first beans in Guatemala, and after experimenting with roasting, de-shelling, grinding and tempering, made his first bars early in 2009. He does not use soya lecithin. He focuses on single-origin, fairly traded chocolate and has high ambition: 'I hope to make the best chocolate in the world'.

Packaging and branding are at an early stage: Duffy's focus is the chocolate. For the moment it is a little confusing that the company name is Red Star, when everyone – Duffy included – calls it Duffy's.

He is one of the new wave of chocolatiers who are willing to be frank about the business. For instance, he makes some bars from cocoa liquor, which brings the cost down slightly. **Star of Peru** is made from cocoa liquor ('single origin, handmade, fairly traded and organic'): the bar is nicely finished in its anonymous mould, typical to all chocolatiers until they are established enough to develop their own identity. It has a good snap and sheen. It also has plenty of

NAME OF THE BAR *Duffy's Corazon del Ecuador Fine Dark Chocolate 72%*
COCOA SOLIDS, BLEND OR ORIGIN *72%, 'single origin artisan chocolate from Ecudaorian Galceta beans'*
INGREDIENTS *Cocoa beans, organic sugar, cocoa butter*
WEIGHT OF BAR *80g*
BAR MADE *Humberston, Lincolnshire, England*
WEBSITE *www.redstarchocolate.co.uk*
AROMA *Berry fruit, citrus, nutty*
TASTE *A burst of citrus is enveloped by a warm coat of earthy, toasty chocolate. The palate is textured but not overly grainy. The citrus comes breaking through again as the chocolate flavours recede to a long, slightly fudgy finish.*

PROFILE

Floral		Nutty	🌸
Fruity	🌸🌸🌸	Spicy	
Winey		Toasty	🌸🌸
Honey	🌸🌸	Smoky	
Creamy	🌸🌸	Earthy	🌸

character, with molasses, bananas, limes, dried fruits, roasted coffee, and a cappuccino milkiness. Only the texture leaves a bit to be desired, but Sheardown's customers may prefer his gritty appeal.

Some of the bars are made in short runs: ' **Heart of Panama** 70% is limited to 200 bars because I have run out of beans'. He spells out disarmingly the complications that go into making chocolate: 'I can't temper any more bars until my mechanic gets back from a course and rebuilds my auction-buy temperer. I could do it by hand on a granite slab ...'

The chocolate world needs more people like Duffy Sheardown: 'I think there is too much mystification going on and people need to just trust their tastebuds a little more.'

Richard Donnelly

During my research for this book, Richard Donnelly's bars lingered on my tasting table. It was simply that they looked so pretty in their colourful packaging that I could not bear to open them. The bars are a handy 45g, not too small, not too large. Wrapped in golden foil paper, and then in handmade paper based on Japanese designs, they are almost too nice to unwrap!

Donnelly set out on his path to chocolate after he realised he was never going to be a lawyer. Instead, he studied in Europe and ended up in Brussels as an apprentice at one of the city's top patisseries, Wittamer. He went next to San Francisco, and was inspired by the chef at La Nouvelle Patisserie. Ready to set up on his own, he began making chocolate in his mother's kitchen in Boston, Massachusetts, and finally established a business in Santa Cruz, California.

Donnelly was one of the first to launch fine chocolate bars on the West Coast, in 1988, and he has remained true to his ideal of small-batch, artisan production. Truffles and ganaches keep him occupied, but he continues with the dark and flavoured bars – **Cinnamon**, **Five Spice**, **Cardamom**, the best-selling **Chipotle**, the particularly good **Almond**, and more. For those who like extremely rich, filled bars, his peanut butter and his hazelnut Gianduja bars are a melting, silken treat, where the chocolate is poured into the moulds first to create the sleekest coating.

NAME OF THE BAR *Richard Donnelly Bittersweet Chocolate*
COCOA SOLIDS, BLEND OR ORIGIN *65%*
INGREDIENTS *Dark chocolate (contains cocoa liquor, sugar, cocoa butter, lecithin as an emulsifier, and vanilla)*
WEIGHT OF BAR *45g*
BAR MADE *Santa Cruz, California, USA*
WEBSITE *www.donnellychocolates.com*
AROMA *Elegantly dark, with finely roasted mocha and floral notes*
TASTE *Silky dark chocolate: develops gently into a creamy richness, with a lift of citrus to refresh the finish.*

PROFILE

Floral		Nutty	🌰🌰
Fruity	🌰🌰🌰	Spicy	🌰
Winey	🌰🌰	Toasty	
Honey	🌰🌰	Smoky	🌰
Creamy		Earthy	🌰

Donnelly is a remarkable figure. First, for his generosity to his chocolate colleagues, cheerfully sending me recommendations of his favourite producers, and new names to look out for. Second, for his other life as 'a semi full time student at UCSC (University of California Santa Cruz) in the undergraduate economics department'. Wait just a few years: Richard Donnelly looks set to become chocolate's first Professor of Economics.

Rococo

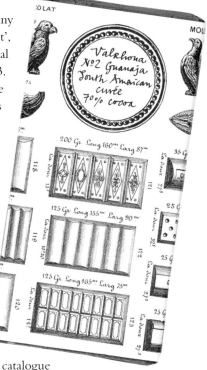

Long before Juliette Binoche and Johnny Depp appeared on screen in 'Chocolat', Chantal Coady had created the ideal chocolate shop fantasy in Rococo in 1983. It was a real achievement, given that she started in London where in those days there was no fine chocolate scene. Nor had she trained as a pastry chef as many other chocolatiers have done. Far more important was the influence of her childhood amid the tastes and flavours of the Middle East, and her training as an art student.

A spell on the chocolate counter of Harrods taught her much, including the importance of packaging. No shopper leaves any of her three stores without a beribboned bag or patterned box. The inspiration for the designs comes from a French catalogue of chocolate moulds of the 1850s.

Coady has a busy trade selling everything from truffles and handpainted chocolate figurines, to sea-salted 'ravioli' and an ever-changing range of ganaches created in the downstairs studio of the Belgravia shop. Her chocolatier is the tall, intense Laurent Couchaux, formerly of the Valrhona Academy. Coady understands her customers well, and knows that while she must have violet creams for some customers, others want entertainment, right down to sleep-over parties for children. Coady and her partner James Booth also do their bit to support cacao, having an interest in a cacao farm on the island of Grenada where their good friend Mott Green at The Grenada Chocolate Company (see page 130) grows cacao and makes chocolate.

NAME OF THE BAR *Rococo Valrhona No 2 Guanaja South American Cuvée 70%*
COCOA SOLIDS, BLEND OR ORIGIN *70%, Caribbean blend*
INGREDIENTS *Cocoa mass, cocoa butter, sugar, soya lecithin, natural vanilla*
WEIGHT OF BAR *85g*
BAR MADE *London, England*
WEBSITE *www.rococochocolates.com*
AROMA *Floral, nutty, red fruits*
TASTE *Supple, creamy and intense, a classic dark bar. The flavours develop into a high roasted mid-palate, with darts of freshness at the heart, with blueberries and redcurrants. Then a gentle decline through waves of mocha and roasted nuts to a clean finish with a bite of tannin.*

PROFILE

Floral	🍂	Nutty	🍂🍂
Fruity	🍂🍂🍂	Spicy	
Winey	🍂	Toasty	🍂🍂
Honey	🍂🍂🍂	Smoky	🍂
Creamy	🍂🍂	Earthy	🍂

Rococo has an intriguing line in flavoured bars, from **Orange and Geranium Dark Chocolate** to **Cardamom White Chocolate** (which goes very well with ultra-sweet wines such as Montilla PX). She is a rare chocolatier who names the couvertures used for some of her bars. Of the plain bars, **Valrhona No 1 Grand Cru Manjari** 64% is a Valrhona classic with a brisk bite of orange (see Valrhona page 216). **Valrhona No 2 Guanaja** is reviewed above.

Rogue

This is a great name for a business. It definitely implies something out of the ordinary. Colin Gasko, based in Minneapolis, is certainly that. He started working in Whole Foods, the world's largest retailer of natural and organic foods, and was soon convinced that he could make chocolate better than anything he was selling. This is the step that is so fascinating. How and why do new artisans take on such a complicated task? As Gasko himself puts it: 'I source the finest cacao and clean, roast, winnow, grind, refine, conche, temper, mold, and package it myself.' He goes on, 'The chocolate you are about to enjoy has kept me up late into the evening and woken me early in the morning for its care.' Chocolate has clearly stepped over from being a fascination to an obsession.

Gasko is still only in his twenties. When building his mini-factory he was fortunate that his father had a background in theoretical physics and was able to help him set up all his machinery, as well as acting as the 'R&D department'. He started making his first bars in late 2007 using cacao from Madagascar's Sambirano Valley; the beans he uses for the Hispaniola bar come from a small co-operative in the Dominican Republic.

Gasko is very excited about his latest bars. The **Rio Caribe** 70% comes from from Venezuela's Paria Peninsula and has a deep, creamy, citrus profile. He also has a small production of a bar from beans from Piura in northern Peru, with a mild, fruity character. A promising beginning for the youngest commercial producer of bars from beans.

NAME OF THE BAR *Rogue Chocolatier Hispaniola 70%*
COCOA SOLIDS, BLEND OR ORIGIN *70%, Dominican Republic*
INGREDIENTS *Cocoa beans, cane sugar, cocoa butter, Tahitian vanilla*
WEIGHT OF BAR *60g*
BAR MADE *Minneapolis, Minnesota, USA*
WEBSITE *www.roguechocolatier.com*
AROMA *Nutty, earthy, roasted*
TASTE *Smooth, supple initial impression as chocolate begins to melt. Flavours build through dark chocolate to tar and liquorice. The finish is refreshed by notes of red wine and citrus.*

PROFILE

Floral		Nutty	🌱
Fruity	🌱	Spicy	🌱🌱
Winey	🌱🌱	Toasty	🌱🌱
Honey	🌱	Smoky	🌱🌱
Creamy	🌱	Earthy	🌱

Rózsavölgyi Csokoládé

The evocatively packaged and presented chocolates produced by the team at Rózsavölgyi Csokoládé recall the glamour of the Austro-Hungarian empire. The little shop in Budapest, decorated with colourful cacao pods at the entrance, seems to be a place where time stands still and indulgence rules.

Take a closer look at the chocolates, though, and there are some radical flavours. This is not a chocolatier that has been frozen in the past. The hot chocolate comes in three flavours: spicy, lavender and green tea. Chilli abounds – in truffles, bars and ganaches. My first encounter with the chocolates was at the Academy of Chocolate Awards in 2009. Taken out of their packaging, the chocolates spoke for themselves, with original, integrated flavours. The **Ancho Chilli & Lemon Oil** won a Silver medal, and the **Raspberry & Cherry Palinka** a Bronze.

The 70% bars are splendidly presented, each moulded into an ornately decorated square that snaps efficiently into smaller pieces. It has the look of a

NAME OF THE BAR *Rózsavölgyi Csokoládé Venezuela 72%*
COCOA SOLIDS, BLEND OR ORIGIN *72% Trincheras*
INGREDIENTS *Cocoa beans, cane sugar*
WEIGHT OF BAR *85g*
BAR MADE *Budapest, Hungary*
WEBSITE *www.rozsavolgyi.com*
AROMA *Earthy with liquorice and aniseed*
TASTE *Starts earthy with black liquorice, but then unexpectedly reveals green apple, pear, Muscat grapes, red liquorice. The texture is grainy and matches the flavours of raw sugar in the mouth. A long rich, savoury finish.*

PROFILE

Floral	🌱		Nutty	🌱🌱
Fruity	🌱🌱		Spicy	🌱🌱
Winey	🌱		Toasty	🌱🌱
Honey	🌱🌱		Smoky	🌱
Creamy	🌱		Earthy	🌱🌱

shortbread mould decorated with Mayan symbols. The chocolate is well-finished with a good sheen. The bars are wrapped in greaseproof paper, and then in a matt, black and white cardboard carton. On closer inspection the carton's design is of cacao pods, and peeping out of the midst of the leaves is a naive face and several birds, two of them eagerly taking the nibs from the pods and flying off with them. The finish and the attention to detail set Rózsavölgyi Csokoládé apart.

The flavoured bars include vanilla, chilli, cardamom and Matcha tea, made with the appropriate origin: Ecuador, the Dominican Republic and Venezuela. There is also a new selection of bean-to-bar chocolate from Venezuelan beans: Carenero, Ocumare, Trincheras and Porcelana.

Scharffen Berger

There are at least three parts to the Scharffen Berger story: the winemaker, the family physician and the giant confectionery company. John Scharffenberger became a very successful winemaker after studying Agricultural Geography at the University of California at Berkeley. He became fascinated by flavours and after selling his wine company spent the next few years working with taste laboratories.

The doctor in the story was a family physician, Robert Steinberg. When he was diagnosed with cancer in 1989, he decided to give up medicine for the pleasures of cooking and eating. His interest in chocolate took him to Bernachon in Lyon (see page 82). In 1996 he set up Scharffen Berger with his friend and former patient Scharffenberger, initially working in his kitchen, where they tasted through 180 samples of beans. Steinberg died in 2008, having seen the company grow from the first 'bean-to-bar' maker in the United States for 50 years to a nationally recognised brand.

The confectionery giant Hershey acquired the business in 2005, at a stroke entering the world of fine chocolate. As the Hershey spokesman put it at the time, 'Scharffen Berger is very on trend'. Whatever the politics of such takeovers, just as with Cadbury's purchase of Green & Black's (see page 128), Hershey has been able to increase the distribution of what was an artisan product.

Scharffenberger, meanwhile, is using his original skills as an agricultural geographer to track down good cacao for sale in limited editions in the Chocolate Maker's Series. **Ben Tre** is a fascinating example in this range because it is one

NAME OF THE BAR *Scharffen Berger Bittersweet Fine Artisan Dark Chocolate 70%*
COCOA SOLIDS, BLEND OR ORIGIN *70%*
INGREDIENTS *Cacao beans, sugar, cocoa butter, non-GMO soy lecithin, whole vanilla beans*
WEIGHT OF BAR *85g*
BAR MADE *Robinson, Illinois, USA*
WEBSITE *www.scharffenberger.com*
AROMA *Red berries, red wine, creamy, nutty*
TASTE *The style is smooth and controlled; a classic Bittersweet. A lightly milky opening develops into coffee, and from there into a broad, fresh blend bright with kumquats and red berries – bitter and sweet. The finish is long and rich, making it a crowd-pleaser.*

PROFILE

Floral	🌶		Nutty	🌶
Fruity	🌶🌶🌶		Spicy	
Winey	🌶🌶🌶		Toasty	🌶
Honey	🌶🌶🌶		Smoky	
Creamy	🌶🌶		Earthy	🌶

of the first bars using beans from Vietnam: very fruity, the flavours include lemon, tangerine and coconut, finely made with a long, smooth, persistent finish. **Asante** from Ghana is supple and creamy, with notes of Parma violets, red fruits and a rounded, tannic signature. **Amina** (named after the wife of a grower) from Madagascar has a creamy character with apricot notes and a firm grip, typical of the origin.

Scharffenberger is full of opinion on the cacao business: 'São Tomé has some of the vilest cacao in the world'; 'Chocolate keeps growers impoverished'; 'I will pay growers three times more than the minimum, while Fairtrade has yet to give me a bar I want to buy'.

The world of chocolate needs individuals like this who challenge accepted practices, and have the influence to do something about it.

Schoc

Roger Simpson and Murray Langham set up Schoc, a chocolate shop and chocolate therapy studio in Greytown, on New Zealand's North Island, in 2002, using the premises of the town's original confectionery shop. Schoc certainly offers a great deal more than a sweet shop, because of the owners' interests in what they call 'gourmet chocolate and self-exploration'.

Murray Langham has a background as a chef and restaurant owner, but he also has diplomas in clinical hypnotherapy, neuro-linguistic programming and counselling. Roger Simpson is an artist qualified in Radical Spiritual Thera-peutics and he also handpaints the chocolate. Not to put too fine a point on it, when you ask for a Pink peppercorn or Smoked paprika flavour they will have a good understanding of the mood you are in. Langham has also written a book on chocolate therapy and Schoc is available for light-hearted pop psy-chology or serious one-to-one consultations.

NAME OF THE BAR *Schoc Santo Domingo 70%*
COCOA SOLIDS, BLEND OR ORIGIN *70%*
INGREDIENTS *Cocoa mass, sugar, cocoa butter, natural vanilla*
WEIGHT OF BAR *80g*
BAR MADE *Greytown, Wairarapa, New Zealand*
WEBSITE *www.schoc.co.nz*
AROMA *Dark mocha with high roast notes*
TASTE *Slow melt, gradual build of flavour to tannic mid-palate; citrus and mint appear with leather and red fruit; slightly hollow, with final toasty notes.*

PROFILE

Floral		Nutty	
Fruity	❦	Spicy	
Winey		Toasty	❦❦
Honey	❦	Smoky	❦
Creamy	❦	Earthy	❦❦

Their truffles and chocolates are brightly coloured and decorated with transfers with the clear intention of cheering up the recipient. Given their proximity to the prime wine-growing region of Martinborough, it is no surprise that Schoc also sells boxes of wine-flavoured truffles.

They make bars in white, milk 33%, dark 53%, bittersweet/bitter 70-100% categories, and six origins: Ecuador 70%, Grenada 60%, Java 33%, Santo Domingo 70% (see profile above), Sao Thome 70% and Tanzania 72%. There are plenty of flavours to distract the indecisive, 22 in all, including **Lime Chilli, Cardamom, Lavender, Strawberry & Black Pepper** and **Rose**. The bars are packed in a form of tobacco pouch – as you open the pouch of the **Rose** bar a few rose petals escape. The bars are well finished, with a good sheen.

Sir Hans Sloane

Chocolate lovers visiting London may find themselves crossing Sloane Square on their way to Artisan du Chocolat (see page 76) or William Curley (see page 222). It is appropriate that they should, since Sir Hans Sloane (1660-1753), after whom the Square is named, is Britain's original chocolate hero. While working in Jamaica as physician to the Governor of the island, Sloane found that adding milk to the local cocoa drink made it more palatable. He brought this recipe back to England, and it was taken up by apothecaries who sold it as a medicine. Sloane was one of the leading intellectuals of his day and became President of the Royal Society and the Royal College of Physicians. After his death, his remarkable private collection of antiquities formed the basis for the British Museum.

Scroll forward some 300 years and the chocolatier behind today's Sir Hans Sloane business is Bill McCarrick, a patissier/chocolatier who has worked around the world, from Australia to Hong Kong, from Bali to Dubai. In 2001 he became head of production, in charge of all bakery, pastry and chocolate, at Harrods in London. In 2006 he swapped this bustling empire for the calmer environment of a studio at Brooklands, south-west of London and famed as the world's first (1907-39) purpose-built motor-racing circuit.

McCarrick was the first artisan producer in the United Kingdom to conch his own chocolate. He created a range of elegant pralines with his couverture. He has also become known for his drinking chocolate, made by spraying sugar grains with a fine mist of cocoa to form a mass of shiny beads. His bars, made

NAME OF THE BAR *Sir Hans Sloane Dark Chocolate*
COCOA SOLIDS, BLEND OR ORIGIN *64%*
INGREDIENTS *Cocoa paste, brown sugar, cocoa butter, Maldon sea salt*
WEIGHT OF BAR *50g*
BAR MADE *Brooklands, Surrey, England*
WEBSITE *www.sirhanssloane.com*
AROMA *Tropically floral and fruity, matching the cacao flowers on the mould*
TASTE *Initially fruity, it develops a fruity, honeyed profile, blossoming to a creamy, jam and berry mid-palate. Lively elegant, citrus finish. The salt is not noticeable; it simply lifts the flavours.*

PROFILE

Floral	🌸🌸	Nutty	🌸
Fruity	🌸🌸	Spicy	
Winey	🌸	Toasty	🌸
Honey	🌸🌸🌸	Smoky	
Creamy	🌸🌸🌸	Earthy	🌸

in moulds embellished with cacao pods, have the sheen and perfect finish of the professional. The flavoured bars are **Mint** (dark) and **Winter Spice** (milk). He also makes bars with the crystallised flavourings studded in the reverse of the bar: **Cranberry & Mandarin** (milk), **Rose Petals** (dark) and **Raspberry** (dark).

In the studio the experimentation continues. McCarrick has now become fascinated with the coarser textures and vibrant character produced in chocolate conched for a short time. Scientist and investigator Sir Hans Sloane has found a worthy heir in Bill McCarrick. In humorous homage to his predecessor, McCarrick has created small chocolate tablets called Sloane Squares.

Above: Sir Hans Sloane (1660–1753) was Britain's original chocolate hero.

T'a

The brothers Tancredi and Alberto
Alemagna have a delightfully Italian
approach to chocolate and their ideal
consumers. Interviewed in Italy soon
after they launched T'a in 2008, they
commented that they were thinking
of a woman rediscovering the
pleasures of chocolate as it used to
be, by nibbling on a little 8g T'a
square, which gave her all the
indulgence in one small bite.
They said they also made chocolate
for men, at 72%, and for children at 40%.

The brothers are the fourth generation of Alemagnas to deliver sweet
nothings to the people of Milan. Casa Alemagna started in 1911, and they
credit their family with inventing panettone, the light, fruited bread, which is
such a favourite at Christmas. However, Signor Motta's descendants might
argue with that. The truth is that for a number of years the Alemagnas and the
Mottas were the two families who dominated the panettone business. Eventually both Casa Alemagna and Motta were bought by Nestlé and then sold on
the Italian company Bauli.

From the outset the Alemagnas wanted the T'a packaging to be as good as the
chocolate – and it is. The chocolates come in elegant card boxes while the
packaging of the bars is delightful. The brightly coloured packs keep the
chocolate free from contamination, and fit neatly into an Armani jacket
pocket or a Lamborghini glove box. T'a is part of the contemporary trend for
square bars; the T'a bars are still small and different enough to be memorable.

The Alemagnas' flavoured bars are all 66%, paired with Calabrian liquorice,
Sorrento lemons or Japanese pepper. They also offer their 72% in a tasting box
with extra virgin olive oil from their estate in Puglia. In addition to the white
and the 40% milk bars, they also make dark bars at 66%, 72% and 80%. They

NAME OF THE BAR *T'a Cioccolato Handmade Fondente 72%*
COCOA SOLIDS, BLEND OR ORIGIN *72%, 'Grand Cru Venezuela, a blend of Trinitario and Criollo'*
INGREDIENTS *Cacao paste, sugar, cocoa butter, powdered whole milk, emulsifier; soy lecithin, natural vanillin*
WEIGHT OF BAR *50g*
BAR MADE *Milan, Italy*
WEBSITE *www.tamilano.com*
AROMA *Green apples, earthy, floral, nutty*
TASTE *The flavour develops slowly, melting to a gently creamy, honeyed core with light notes of milky chocolate and orange peel; very gradually a grip of tannin builds to a short finish with a firm, dry end. The texture is smooth and finely grained.*

PROFILE

Floral		Nutty	✿✿
Fruity	✿✿	Spicy	✿
Winey	✿	Toasty	✿✿
Honey	✿✿✿	Smoky	✿
Creamy	✿✿	Earthy	✿✿✿

source beans from Mexico, Venezuela, Ecuador, Colombia, Brazil, Ghana and Tanzania for both their origin bars and blends. The Alemagnas are chocolatiers who value pleasure, adding milk powder to their bars, even the 80%. Along with the soya lecithin and the vanillin, the milk powder undoubtedly smoothes the palate and makes for a fuller, fudgier sensation as it melts.

To return to the image of Italian fashion, this is chocolate dressed in a warm fur coat; there are other Italian chocolates in this book dressed in linen or in silk. All of them glamorous – the choice is yours.

Taza

Taza is one of the small but slowly increasing band of bean-to-bar producers in the United States. Co-founder Alex Whitmore, raised on European-style confectionery chocolate, discovered the tradition of stoneground cacao on a trip to Oaxaca in Mexico. He saw how the beans were pounded on a stone *metate* – like a pestle and mortar – just as they have been for centuries. He tasted the powerful, real chocolate flavour and the grainy texture, and was inspired to set up a business to produce artisan organic chocolate with the original flavour of Mexico.

Whitmore – a former anthropology student, parachute packer and fleet manager of the car-sharing service, Zipcar – and his business partner, Larry Slotnick – one-time engineer and silversmith, also ex-Zipcar – set up their business in 2006, and the first bars were made in Whitmore's kitchen. They subsequently established a factory in Somerville, Massachusetts. Whitmore and Slotnick were determined to run their business on what they define as 'direct trade' terms, paying producers over the odds, and creating relationships with the growers which were financially and environmentally stable.

NAME OF THE BAR *Taza Stone Ground Organic Chocolate 60% Dark*
COCOA SOLIDS, BLEND OR ORIGIN *60%, Dominican Republic, organic*
INGREDIENTS *Cacao beans, cane sugar, cocoa butter, whole vanilla beans*
WEIGHT OF BAR *85g*
BAR MADE *Somerville, Massachusetts, USA*
WEBSITE *www.tazachocolate.com*
AROMA *Floral and spicy with red fruits*
TASTE *The first impression is grainy, suggesting the stone grinding. This is followed by a surprisingly sweet palate of lime cordial and vanilla, and backnotes of chocolate with a hint of bitterness.*

PROFILE

Floral		Nutty	❦
Fruity	❦❦❦	Spicy	❦
Winey	❦❦❦	Toasty	
Honey	❦	Smoky	❦
Creamy	❦	Earthy	

Taza has gathered together the usual panoply of necessary equipment, winnowers, roasters and conches, much of it secondhand, as is typical of these new bean-to-bar artisans. One piece of kit, the stone mill, makes Taza's chocolate different. Whitmore studied with a stone miller in Oaxaca, and uses Mexican hand-hewn granite millstones to grind the nibs to a grainy paste.

Taza's first product was discs of chocolate for shaving into water or milk for drinking chocolate. The drink is served in a 'taza', or cup, hence the name of the company. Taza now produce discs in a riot of herb and spice flavours including yerba maté.

There are now three regular dark bars – 60% (see profile above), 70% and 80% – as well as short-run limited editions, such as a special purchase from Mexico, made from beans from Soconusco in Chiapas. There are also indulgences, such as chocolate-coated almonds and nibs.

Tcho

Silicon Valley collides headlong with old-school chocolate at Tcho, San Francisco's only chocolate factory (at Pier 17). Tcho is a remarkable combination of wholesome cocoa with glamorous design and IT language, talking of its 'operating heuristics' (values), 'beta chocolate' (trial samples), '1.0' (launch editions), and even moulding its bars and wrapping them in 'algorithmic guilloché patterns'.

The language comes easily because one of the founders, Timothy Childs, was a software engineer on NASA's space shuttle programme, while the other, Karl Bittong, had a long history in cacao and chocolate. The style is undoubtedly driven by CEO Louis Rossetto, one of the founders of *Wired* magazine. Together with Brad Kintzer, a cacao expert formerly with Scharffen Berger (see page 200) who has worked with other leading chocolatiers such as Michael Recchiuti, they make a great team.

Tcho (pronounced 'choh') is not just technospeak; it emphasises that it is obsessive about chocolate, and that it also has a commitment to equitable working and assisting the growers with improving their practices. Some of the bars are already fair trade. All the bars carry the words 'No slavery', to draw attention to its continued existence in some cacao-growing regions, and to indicate that Tcho refuses 'to use cacao produced by slaves'.

Tcho currently produces four organic dark bars, all well-finished. Each bar is identified by a dominant flavour from Tcho's 'flavor wheel', with the names chosen to indicate the inherent character of the chocolate, not any added ingredients. **Chocolatey** comes from Ghana (see profile facing page), **Citrus**

NAME OF THE BAR *Tcho Dark Chocolate 'Chocolatey' Ghana 70%*
COCOA SOLIDS, BLEND OR ORIGIN *70%, Ghana*
INGREDIENTS *Cacao beans, cane sugar, cocoa butter, soy lecithin, vanilla beans*
WEIGHT OF BAR *60g*
BAR MADE *San Francisco, California, USA*
WEBSITE *www.tcho.com*
AROMA *Expressive: balsamic, earthy, citrus*
TASTE *Comfortingly chocolatey at the outset, a real dark brown warmth; very slowly a bright, clean dart of citrus comes through to lift the enveloping weight of the chocolate. The melt is rich and fudgy, though it lacks the lively freshness of Tcho's other bars. Long, dense finish.*

PROFILE

Floral		Nutty	🌰🌰
Fruity	🌰🌰🌰	Spicy	🌰
Winey		Toasty	🌰🌰
Honey	🌰🌰🌰	Smoky	🌰
Creamy	🌰🌰🌰	Earthy	🌰

from Madagascar, **Fruity** from Peru and **Nutty** from Ecuador. There are plans in train for milk chocolate bars, too.

The website is worth a visit, with plenty of information about the company. There are also some recipes: amid the brownies and cheesecakes, look out for something completely different – bison steak with cocoa nib sauce.

Theo

Theo's claim to fame is being the first producer in the United States to make organic and Fair Trade chocolate. Founder Joe Whinney worked in the tropical rainforests of Central America and Africa in the 1990s, and set up a project to export organic cocoa beans to North America. This was undoubtedly partly driven by his own personal liking for chocolate. He also saw that it was a way of developing a fair trade with the growers, giving them a more equitable return for their beans. A decade later, after research and planning, he moved to Seattle and converted the historic Redhook brewery in the Fremont district into the Theo chocolate factory. Theo made its first chocolate in 2006.

Theo's Fairtrade cacao comes from a number of sources, including the Côte d'Ivoire. This is an important point because it means that by buying a brand like Theo it is possible to eat Côte d'Ivoire chocolate without the taint of slave labour. Theo may be fair trade and organic, but it is also fun. There are delicate ganaches flavoured with scented teas, as well as over-the-top 'Big Daddy' chocolates: substantial chocolate-coated cubes, with marshmallow or peanut butter praline layered on caramel and Graham crackers. The marshmallow is decorated with a smoked milk chocolate swirl, the peanut butter with chopped peanuts.

For the traditionalist, Theo offers classic flavoured bars: **Mint**, **Spicy Chile**, **Cherry & Almond** and **Orange**, all of them in 70% dark chocolate. The Fantasy flavoured selection includes the overwhelmingly spicy **Coconut Curry** milk bar, **Bread & Chocolate**, **Nib Brittle**, and my favourite, the imaginatively fruity **Fig, Fennel & Almond**. In the plain bars, Theo makes a 45% milk and a 70% **Rich** dark (see profile facing page), as well as single-

NAME OF THE BAR *Theo Organic Fair Trade Rich Dark Chocolate 70%*
COCOA SOLIDS, BLEND OR ORIGIN *70%*
INGREDIENTS *Organic and Fair trade cocoa beans, sugar, cocoa butter, organic ground vanilla bean*
WEIGHT OF BAR *84g*
BAR MADE *Seattle, Washington State, USA*
WEBSITE *www.theochocolate.com*
AROMA *Earthy, balsamic, leafy*
TASTE *Creamy, mocha appeal; opens out into a mouthful of broad chocolatey flavours. The finish is quite short with a bite of earthy tannin.*

PROFILE

Floral	🍃		Nutty	🍃
Fruity	🍃🍃		Spicy	
Winey	🍃		Toasty	
Honey	🍃🍃🍃		Smoky	
Creamy	🍃🍃🍃		Earthy	🍃

origin **Madagascar** (74%), **Ghana** (84%) and **Costa Rica** (91%). There are also two bars that raise funds for the work of the conservationist Dr Jane Goodall, a 45% milk and a 70% dark, helping both cacao growers and conservation work with chimpanzees in tropical rainforests.

Theo is keen to encourage its customers to hold chocolate parties. They have put together 'pairing kits' of origin and flavoured bars to try with wines or beers. In a version of the classic curry and lager combo, the beer pack includes the unforgettable **Coconut Curry** bar.

Thorntons

The tale of 'How Thorntons Rediscovered Chocolate Bars' sounds like a charming children's fable with the sugary sweetener of chocolate in the title. In fact, it is a vivid portrayal of the way attitudes to chocolate have changed, and how rapidly.

Thorntons was originally founded in Sheffield, South Yorkshire, a century ago, but later moved its base to Derbyshire. The company

won a deserved reputation for making Swiss- and Belgian-style chocolates, but with an all-English spin, typified in their 'Continental' collection. As the power of the big chocolate brands grew, Thorntons nevertheless managed to keep the loyalty of its consumers.

However, as with most things, fashions change. The multinational company Cadbury recognised this when it bought Green & Black's (see page 128) in 2009, giving it a ready-made quality chocolate bar business with an environmentally friendly image. Thorntons, with its special boxed collections and homely toffees, had never needed to specialise in 'boring' bars. Now it had to catch up – and catch up it has. It brought in chocolatier Keith Hurdman, who had long experience working at Felchlin in Switzerland, and more recently with Louise Nason at Melt (see page 164). Hurdman knew where to source fine couvertures, and in due course he came up with an impressive collection of bars in tune with contemporary fashions.

The bars are 70g square blocks. Square is still a relatively unusual shape for chocolate bars, but it is user-friendly and memorable. In the range, Hurdman has produced some good bars at competitive prices. His award winners include a **Venezuela** 38% milk, a **Tonka** bean 38% (surely one of the first bars in mainstream production made from this fragrant seed) and a **Lightly Salted**

NAME OF THE BAR *Thorntons Dark Chocolate French 70%*
COCOA SOLIDS, BLEND OR ORIGIN *70%*
INGREDIENTS *Dark chocolate made in France: Cocoa mass, sugar, emulsifier (soya lecithin),
natural flavouring*
WEIGHT OF BAR *90g*
BAR MADE *Alfreton, Derbyshire, England*
WEBSITE *www.thorntons.co.uk*
AROMA *Dark cocoa, balsamic, violets, citrus*
TASTE *A rich melt, bright with coconut, smooth and creamy; the mid-palate is also rich with
lightly toasted mocha; gentle citrus notes follow through on the finish*

PROFILE

Floral		Nutty	🌶🌶
Fruity	🌶	Spicy	
Winey	🌶	Toasty	🌶
Honey	🌶🌶	Smoky	🌶
Creamy	🌶🌶🌶	Earthy	🌶

Macadamia 60% dark. Inevitably, the range has been swelled with more commercial flavours such as **Strawberry** milk chocolate and Belgian **White**. Even so, some of these bars, such as the **85% dark**, the **Balsamic** dark chocolate and the **Orange & Cardamom** will be a revelation to consumers new to the world of fine chocolate. Packaged in striking colours, these blocks form an excellent introduction to the changing world of chocolate.

Valrhona

When was the last time you bought a Valrhona chocolate bar? Last week? Last year? Never? However, if you have ever eaten a chocolate dessert in an elegant European restaurant, the chances are the chocolate will have been Valrhona. It is one of the two chocolate producers that regularly gets a name check on the menu – 'Valrhona souf-flé'. (The other is Amedei, see page 70.) Most of the top chocolatiers in this book use Valrhona as a couverture at least some of the time, though they may not advertise the fact.

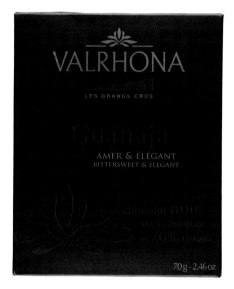

Valrhona has come to dominate the market because of its unique combination of relative availability and affordability, with fine quality.

Valrhona comes from France's Rhône Valley and was founded in 1922 as the Chocolaterie du Vivarais; it changed its name in 1947. In the mid-1980s it was acquired by food conglomerate Bongrain, and there are regular rumours that a major chocolate company wants to take them over.

Valrhona can claim a number of firsts: it was among the first to sell Grand Cru chocolate – chocolate from a single origin; the first of which was Guanaja, named after the Caribbean island where Columbus first encountered cacao. It was also among the first to create a demand for 70% cocoa solids and to produce vintage chocolates, from a named year. Valrhona origins have become standards: **Guanaja** (created in 1986) was originally sold as 'the bitterest chocolate in the world' (see facing page); **Manjari**, at 64%, is a classic dark bar from Madagascar. **Caraïbe** 66% and **Jivara** 40% milk are well-established popular blends.

NAME OF THE BAR *Valrhona Guanaja dark chocolate 70%*
COCOA SOLIDS, BLEND OR ORIGIN *70%, Caribbean blend*
INGREDIENTS *Cocoa beans, sugar, cocoa butter, emulsifier (soya lecithin),
natural vanilla extract*
WEIGHT OF BAR *70g*
BAR MADE *Tain l'Hermitage, Drôme, France*
WEBSITE *www.valrhona.com*
AROMA *Floral and fragrant with tangerines and red fruit*
TASTE *A confidently supple, smooth and refreshing bar, a model of bittersweet. The start is
chocolate and citrus, building to a finely balanced blend of cream and honey covering over the tart
bite of citrus acidity. Elegant fade to a long finish.*

PROFILE

Floral	🍫🍫		Nutty	🍫🍫
Fruity	🍫🍫🍫		Spicy	🍫
Winey	🍫		Toasty	🍫🍫
Honey	🍫🍫		Smoky	🍫
Creamy	🍫🍫		Earthy	🍫

As a business Valrhona takes flavour as seriously as does a good winemaker; and, it is sometimes said, they take themselves as seriously as France's most powerful châteaux owners. Many chocolatiers have anecdotes about difficulties they have had working with the company. But, in their defence, Valrhona is committed to quality, and is determined to hold on to its market.

For a chocolate lover wanting to learn more about styles and origins, Valrhona's Grands Crus are a very good place to start. The extra dark **Abinao**, at 85%, has the Valrhona texture, but lacks real charm. At the other extreme **Tanariva**, at 33%, proves that it is possible to make an (admittedly mild) milk bar that evens wins the approval of chocolate snobs.

Of the flavoured bars, **Manjari Orange** is particularly good, and I find it a good choice when matching chocolate and wine: I pair it regularly with a Banyuls with citrussy highlights, a fortified wine from Roussillon, or with a fortified Malbec from Argentina. I have even had some success matching it with a beer with orangey hops. The **Guanaja Grué** (with Nibs) is also a successful extension of Guanaja flavours.

Vanini

Vanini is the glamorous, fine chocolate brand of the ICAM chocolate group. ICAM (Industria Cioccolato e Affini Morbegno) is one of the behind-the-scenes businesses, like those listed on page 228, that provides chocolate ingredients for caterers, patissiers and chocolatiers. It was founded in 1942 by Silvio Agostini, and in the period of reconstruction in Italy after the Second World War, Agostini and his wife Carolina Vanini, and her brothers, specialised in confectionery and desserts. Gradually they transformed themselves into chocolate specialists, also supplying cocoa butter and cocoa powder to producers. Today, among their range of activities, they are one of the largest producers of organic chocolate and supply organic and Fairtrade chocolate to a number of well-known brands worldwide.

Of their flavoured bars the **Mandorla** (almond) is classic, and the **Fico** (Fig) and **Amarena** (black cherry) are more orig-inal; all are finely balanced against the background of the 49% milk chocolate. The minced black cherry, chewy and slightly sour, is a lively contrast to the milky chocolate. The fig bar is particularly enjoyable for someone who enjoys the interest that texture provides. The figs are the small Turkish ones; their flesh is minced and lightly chewy. The surprise comes only slowly, when the tiny, crunchy seeds escape from their chocolate coating and fill the mouth – and the teeth.

In the plain bar collection Vanini has a 49% **Cacao Intenso**, a high cocoa content for milk chocolate, and four single origin bars, to each of which they suggest a drink pairing: **Madagascar** 70% (Banyuls), **Peru** 70% (Chinato – a herb-infused wine),

NAME OF THE BAR *Vanini Cioccolato Fondente Extra da Singola Origine Piura con Cacao Criollo Peru 70%*

COCOA SOLIDS, BLEND OR ORIGIN *70%, 'from the Hunacabamba province, Piura, Peru'*

INGREDIENTS *Peru cacao 64%, sugar, cocoa butter, natural flavour of vanilla*

WEIGHT OF BAR *75g*

BAR MADE *Lecco, Italy*

WEBSITE *www.vaninicioccolato.it*

AROMA *Richly chocolatey, honeyed and nutty*

TASTE *The melt is slow and gentle. Mangoes and ripe tropical fruits appear, followed by a squeeze of lime, until a firm savoury blast of tannin steps in and takes over. Richly chocolatey on the palate but a little dry.*

PROFILE

Floral		Nutty	❦❦	
Fruity	❦❦❦	Spicy		
Winey	❦❦	Toasty		
Honey	❦❦❦	Smoky	❦❦	
Creamy	❦	Earthy	❦❦❦	

Dominicana (Dominican Republic) 75% (single malt whisky) and **Ecuador** 73% (Pineau des Charentes). All these bars are well finished, with a good shine. The Dominican Republic bar, despite its higher cocoa solids, is surprisingly chocolatey and satisfying, and the expected bite of tannin at the end comes through gently. It is definitely a good accompaniment to a single malt whisky.

Vivani

Vivani is a German chocolate company with an Italian name. It is the organic brand of Ludwig Weinrich, a bakery established in Herford, between Dusseldorf and Hannover, in Germany in 1895. During the 20th century Weinrich transformed itself into a supplier of couvertures and filled chocolates. Vivani was launched in 2000 at Bio Fach, Germany's largest organic fair. Vivani has taken an interest in the ethical production of cacao, working with the Kuapa Kokoo co-operative for Fairtrade (see Divine, page 112), and is now making organic chocolate, for which they say they also pay a premium to their growers. As newcomers to the organic world, they are aware that they need to make organic chocolate that is just as good as any of their other bars.

In line with their commitment to organic production, Vivani use no genetically modified ingredients, no soya lecithin, only real Bourbon vanilla, raw cane sugar and high cocoa solids. There is a full repertoire of organic treats for every age, from chocolate spread and drinking chocolate, to chocolate-coated coffee beans. There is a range of bars to charm children and there are slightly more serious flavoured bars for adults: **Orange** 70%, **Nougat** 70%, **Chilli** 70% and **Cappuccino**, a blend of milk and white chocolate.

Among the plain bars there is a 32% milk and a 37% Ecuador milk, an Ecuador 70%, and the house dark blend at 72%.

NAME OF THE BAR *Vivani Feine Bitter Organic Dark 72%*
COCOA SOLIDS, BLEND OR ORIGIN *72%, organic*
INGREDIENTS *Organic cocoa mass, raw cane sugar, cocoa butter*
WEIGHT OF BAR *100g*
BAR MADE *Herford, Germany*
WEBSITE *www.vivani.de*
AROMA *Earthy, balsamic, roasted mocha notes*
TASTE *Slow to melt, it builds through layers of dark caramel and fudge to a broad, rich chocolate profile with roasted walnuts. The descent to the finish is slow, finally revealing a well-disguised note of bitterness. A reliable, bitter blend.*

PROFILE

Floral		Nutty	🍂🍂
Fruity	🍂🍂	Spicy	🍂
Winey	🍂	Toasty	🍂🍂
Honey	🍂🍂🍂	Smoky	🍂
Creamy	🍂🍂	Earthy	🍂🍂

Weinrich has recently launched the Björnsted collection of chocolate bars (*www.bjoernsted.de*). These are sourced from small growers in South America; like Vivani, these bars are also organic, also made without soya lecithin and sweetened with raw cane sugar.

William Curley

Britain's most precise and subtle chocolatier set up shop in London in 2004, but to the surprise of many he is, in fact, from Scotland, where citizens are rumoured to eat deep-fried chocolate confectionery. From Fife he worked his way up through the kitchens of some of the greatest restaurants in Scotland and England, until he came to be regarded by his peers as the top chefs' patissier/chocolatier. The Academy of Chocolate awarded him Best British Chocolatier in 2007, 2008 and 2009.

His wife Suzue is Japanese, from Osaka, and the couple met when working at London's Savoy Hotel. Together they have represented Scotland in many international culinary events. Their first shop was a tiny boutique in Richmond in south-west London. There was a continuous stream of pilgrims to the shop, including many visitors from Japan. After a brief flirtation with The Chocolate Society, Curley finally opened up a second shop in Pimlico, in central London, in 2009, just around the corner from Artisan du Chocolat (see page 76).

If the intimacy of the delightful Richmond store is lost in Pimlico, at least it is possible to sit down and savour a coffee and a cake. For Curley is still a patissier, and one of his skills is to use chocolate in its lightest possible form, combining it with fruits, or mousses or sponges, or all three.

NAME OF THE BAR *William Curley House Dark 70%*
COCOA SOLIDS, BLEND OR ORIGIN *70%*
INGREDIENTS *Cocoa mass, cane sugar, cocoa butter, vanilla*
WEIGHT OF BAR *50g*
BAR MADE *London, England*
WEBSITE *www.williamcurley.co.uk*
AROMA *Confidently chocolatey, creamy with notes of vanilla*
TASTE *At the beginning the flavour is simply pure and delicate, then it rapidly develops red fruits, with bright notes of rhubarb and a squeeze of citrus, plus a burst of liquorice. The flavours continue to develop and extend, finally slowing down into a cool, almost minty finish. Very complex.*

PROFILE

Floral		Nutty	🌿
Fruity	🌿🌿🌿	Spicy	🌿
Winey	🌿🌿🌿	Toasty	🌿
Honey	🌿	Smoky	🌿
Creamy	🌿🌿🌿	Earthy	🌿

The chocolates too are the epitome of delicacy. The ganaches, in particular, have haunting flavours and technical excellence. The couverture is very thin and the flavours – such as Japanese black vinegar, toasted sesame or yuzu – arrive slowly to surprise and delight.

Curley has become a UK ambassador for Amedei (see page 70), and his shops are good places to see chocolate transformed into ganaches and bars. The bars are all made from Amedei chocolate, to which Curley brings his own technical and creative skill. In the plain range there is white, a milky caramelly **Milk 32%**, **House Dark** 65% and **House Dark** 70% (see profile above). The flavoured range consists of **White Raspberry**, **Milk Cinnamon** and **Dark Chilli**. There are also 150g gift bars studded with fruit and nuts, and **Sea Salt Caramel** and **Praline Feuillantine** filled bars.

Willie's Delectable Cacao

Chocolate producers owe a certain debt to the irrepressible Willie Harcourt-Cooze. Those who saw his television series in 2009 learnt that cacao grows on trees in tropical climates, that the harvesting and processing were fraught with difficulty, and that once the beans were in the factory there was still plenty that could go wrong. For Harcourt-Cooze they did. President Chavez of Venezuela had obviously watched the series and decided that this errant Englishman was taking

too much profit from the land. In the end there was no case to be found against him or the way he treated his workers, but the threats proved again the fragility of supply of the world's best cacao.

Harcourt-Cooze's progression to chocolatier took a winding path. From a country childhood in Ireland, he came to London to study, where he was set upon and stabbed. His life took a few odd turns after that but eventually, some 10 years later, he and his wife bought an estate in the very best cacao zone in the world, the Henri Pittier national park on the north coast of Venezuela, not far from Chuao. He was able to replant the property with Criollo trees and eventually to start up a factory near his home in Devon.

The television series showed only too clearly the many travails of cacao production. In 1998 Harcourt-Cooze started making 100% cacao for the local people in Venezuela. It was made in cylinders for the simple reason that he had a pipe to hand to use as a mould. A decade later he launched the cylinders in Europe for use in cooking and drinking chocolate. Then after plenty of good advice he came up with the idea of producing two square bars: 'one for now', 'one for then', each 40g, packaged in a small chunky box with the words 'tuck in' on the

NAME OF THE BAR *Willie's Delectable Cacao Peruvian 70*
COCOA SOLIDS, BLEND OR ORIGIN *70%, San Martin Province, Peru*
INGREDIENTS *Cocoa mass, cocoa butter, Cuban raw cane sugar*
WEIGHT OF BAR *80g (2 x 40g bars)*
BAR MADE *Uffculme, Devon, England*
WEBSITE *www.williescacao.com*
AROMA *Vibrant: floral, with red wine and bananas*
TASTE *The opening notes suggest little of the wild lively character to come. First appears molasses from the sugar, then flavours pile in of kumquat, apricot, guava, with brisk bitterness underneath. The flavours stay alive in the mouth, and the finish is firmly tannic, with a grainy melt.*

PROFILE

Floral	🍂		Nutty	🍂
Fruity	🍂🍂🍂		Spicy	🍂
Winey			Toasty	🍂🍂🍂
Honey	🍂		Smoky	🍂🍂
Creamy	🍂		Earthy	🍂🍂🍂

inside flap. The range of bars now includes **Venezuelan Rio Caribe Superior 72%**, **Venezuelan Las Trincheras 72%**, **Peruvian San Martin 70%** (profiled above), **Madagascar Sambirano 71%** and **Javan Light Breaking 69%**.

The name of the brand has inevitable comparisons with Willie Wonka, from Roald Dahl's *Charlie and the Chocolate Factory*. The chocolate is too wild and expressive to be a Wonka-ish product. Technically the bars are still a little rugged and grainy, and Willie's was the only sample that arrived on my tasting table with bloom. Nevertheless, in flavour terms, the bars are 'alive'.

Zotter

There can be no better place to finish this A–Z than with Zotter. For Josef Zotter has ideas and personality enough to fill any gaps that remain in the chocolate world. Decorated wrappers, different shapes and sizes, trials with conching, good humour, fascinating blends – Zotter has them all. Zotter is a bean-to-bar family business that has been making chocolate bars since 1985.

There is a riot of no less than 150 flavours in a collection called 'Handscooped' because of the way the fillings are layered up. I was immediately drawn to the outrageous-sounding **Bergkäse, Walnüsse, Trauben,** a blend of Austrian mountain cheese, walnuts, grapes, almonds and a dash of balsamic apple vinegar dipped in dark chocolate. In fact, it was a subtle, sweet bar with more than a hint of marzipan, not in the least cheesy, just right for von Trapp family picnics in 'The Sound of Music'. The flavours go on – **Lemon Polenta,** Bird's **Eye Chilli, Hempseed and Mocha,** Pink Grapefruit with Cashew Kernels and **Schilcher** (an acidic Austrian wine) and the **Pumpkin.** Not every flavour succeeds, but they are definitely fun to try.

Zotter sources beans from Panama, Nicaragua, Peru, Bolivia, Ecuador, Brazil and the Dominican Republic, and all its raw materials suppliers are certified organic and Fairtrade.

There is a delightful CD-sized range of discs of chocolate called **Mitzi Blue** with a wide choice of flavours. **Labooko** is the main label for the 35g single-origin bars, which are packed in pairs. While other producers pack pairs of bars to enjoy at different times, Zotter wants to show how different the same chocolate can be. In the Brazil pack, there is a 70% and a 60% bar from two

NAME OF THE BAR *Zotter Labooko Peru 70%, 20-hour conch and 16-hour conch*
COCOA SOLIDS, BLEND OR ORIGIN *70%, Satipo Pangoa, Peru*
INGREDIENTS *Fairtrade organic cocoa mass, Fairtrade organic cocoa butter, Fairtrade organic raw cane sugar, salt*
WEIGHT OF BAR *70g (2 x 35g)*
BAR MADE *Bergl, Austria*
WEBSITE *www.zotter.at*
AROMA *An excellent illustration of the choices a chocolatier can make with the same beans: 20-hour conch: red wine, cocoa, cream   16-hour conch: earthy, balsamic*
TASTE *20-hour conch: a delicate smooth melt; warm and creamy with red wine and toast highlights, with a long, clean floral finish.*
16-hour conch: more dense and bold with a nutty profile and dry finish.

PROFILES 20-hour conch/16-hour conch

Floral	❦❦/0		Nutty	0/❦❦
Fruity	❦❦❦/❦❦		Spicy	0/0
Winey	❦/❦		Toasty	0/❦❦❦
Honey	❦❦/❦		Smoky	0/❦
Creamy	❦/❦❦		Earthy	❦/❦

regions. The bars are real contrasts: the 60% showing ca0ppuccino and nutmeg, the 70% pepper and spice. The 60% is the mid-morning bar to the 70% for evening. Labooko also has stand-alone bars. How could one not like the Peru 70%, of which Zotter says: 'the cocoa beans are like the people – mild and refined, lending the blend an air of nobility'? Zotter may be a chocolatier, but part of him is a poet, too.

B to B: Bean to Bar or Business to Business

The Directory in the preceding pages celebrates the determination and diversity of today's fine chocolatiers. Yet as one producer said to me, 'there is an enormous amount of smoke and mirrors in the small-scale chocolate industry'. He was referring to the sometimes deliberate confusion over who makes what and where. At present only a small number of producers make chocolate from the bean, in other words 'bean to bar'. The large majority make chocolate 'business to business'. That is to say, they buy finished chocolate, known as couverture, from a chocolate business and melt it, blend it and temper it to create and mould their own bars and chocolate. This takes real skill. To recognise how easy it is to get this wrong, think of the cheap chocolate, melted and moulded from poor couverture, that souvenir shops around the world sell to unsophisticated tourists.

The couverture chocolatiers choose depends on the character they seek, their quality needs and also on the cost. In many cases, producers do not wish to reveal where their chocolate comes from. If they do, they may risk criticism from their colleagues for skimping on cheap couverture. As consumers, we may also criticise a chocolatier for not using a producer that we recognise. Of course if they do not confess, then their competitors will try to catch them out and guess the supplier anyway.

A few well-known suppliers of couverture, who sell chocolate to other chocolatiers and to patissiers, are included in the Chocolate Directory. They have a high profile, and sell directly to consumers. This group includes Amedei, El Rey, ICAM (featured here under Vanini), Kaoka, Michel Cluizel and Valrhona. Of these, Amedei is very highly rated but regarded as too expensive to be used regularly except by a few. Valrhona is probably the most well-known to the chocolate industry, providing an impressive range of industry-standard origin couvertures. Valrhona's chef school has been influential in its work with many top chocolatiers, including Marc Demarquette (see page 110) and Laurent Couchaux at Rococo (see page 194).

More or less hidden from public view, though a few have been mentioned in these pages, are names such as Barry Callebaut (Belgium), Belcolade (Belgium), Chocolaterie de l'Opéra (France), Chocovic (Spain), Felchlin (Switzerland) and Fenix (Argentina). Barry Callebaut started out as Callebaut in 1850 and began its couverture business in 1925. This grew quickly and eventually started to supply large manufacturers with couverture in liquid form delivered by tankers. Through the 1980s Callebaut survived a number of takeovers, and finally in 1997 it merged with Cacao Barry to become one of the world's largest producers of chocolate and chocolate ingredients. Cacao Barry had developed a particular relationship with chefs, patissiers and bakers; it makes special recipe couvertures for many of the best-known names in chocolate. The words Barry Callebaut may not roll off our lips as consumers, but its products undoubtedly pass our lips.

Chocolaterie de l'Opéra offers its professional customers plantation chocolates, thanks to the efforts of Olivier de Loisy and his passion for sourcing Les Pures Plantations. In today's world of origin chocolates, it is easy to forget the pioneering efforts of aficionados like de Loisy. He is particularly good at describing the different styles and characters of his origins. His book, *Chocolat et Grands Crus de Cacao*, written with Katherine Khodorowsky, is an enjoyable, informed introduction to the subject. Felchlin is another supplier of top-quality couverture and it has been working with a number of chocolatiers featured in these pages who are keen to discover the potential of their beans. In all of these companies, the consultancy and technical advice they give is an important part of the relationship. The problem for a new chocolatier today is not finding premises, or sourcing couverture, or designing a label – the difficulty is finding reliable, disinterested advice.

Other Producers

A number of fascinating and interesting producers did not make the final pages. All of these are well worth seeking out.

Cocoa Rhapsody (Australia)
www.cocoarhapsody.com.au
Fair trade, organic cacao from the Dominican Republic, 72-hour conch. Vegan-friendly chocolate.

Coppeneur (Germany)
www.coppeneurchocolate.com
'We recently became the first micro-batch bean-to-bar producer in Germany.'

Damian Allsop (England)
www.damianallsop.com
Very creative chocolatier, specialising in pure flavoured ganaches made with water rather than cream. Fun, flavoured 'Compact bars': discs of chocolate packed in CD cases.

De Vries Chocolate (USA)
www.devrieschocolate.com
One of the new generation of bean-to-bar pioneers in the United States.

El Ceibo (Bolivia) *www.elceibo.org*
A co-operative in the Alto Beni region of Bolivia.

Ghirardelli (USA)
www.ghirardelli.com
The USA's 'longest continuously operating chocolate manufacturer'. Bean-to-bar maker.

Jacques Torres (USA)
www.mrchocolate.com
Makes a 70% bar from African and South American beans.

Recchiuti (USA)
www.recchiuti.com
Engaging, committed, experienced producer of bars and plenty more.

Glossary

Alcohol Chocolate and alcohol are not great bedfellows, and chocolate bars are particularly difficult matches. Red and white table wines (under 15% ABV) rarely work. Fortified wines, and spirits, from 16% ABV upwards can be more successful. For more information, see page 59.

Antioxidants Compounds that reduce the effects of oxidation of unstable molecules in the body, a process which can release damaging free radicals. Found in a wide selection of foods, among them green tea, red wine and cocoa. See also page 29.

Bean to bar Shorthand phrase for producers who manage production starting with the bean, usually the fermented, dried cocoa beans, through to the finished bar. Some producers work with the cacao in the place of origin, and oversee harvest, fermentation and drying.

Bittersweet No legal definition. A dark chocolate, usually over 50% cocoa solids.

Bloom The white powder or sheen on chocolate. Either the chocolate has become too warm and the cocoa butter has risen to the surface, and then crystallised; or the chocolate has become moist (typically in a fridge) and the sugar has come to the surface and crystallised.

Bonbon A fruit, nut, fondant or other filled centre dipped in chocolate.

Cacao ('ka-kow') The name given to the tree, its pods and the unfermented beans. Cocoa is the word to describe the beans after fermenting and roasting, and all the subsequent by-products such as nibs, powder and butter.

Carob Made from the pods of the carob tree, *Ceratonia siliqua*, often known as locust beans. Long used for animal feed, but in the past 50 years or so has become a fashionable health food, partly because it contains no caffeine, cholesterol, theobromine or oxalic acid. Carob is very sweet, but only 0.7% fat. It is possible to learn to love carob on its own terms, but do not think of it as chocolate.

Carré, napolitain, palet A small, individually wrapped square of chocolate.

Chocolatier A small-batch producer of chocolates, often also a producer of fine patisserie.

Cocoa bean The bean from inside the pod, which is the fruit of the cacao tree. Once fermented and dried, it can be roasted and the husk winnowed off to release the cocoa nibs.

Cocoa butter The fat found within the nibs of the cocoa beans, around 50-55% of the bean. Obtained by pressing the beans after they have been roasted and their husks removed in a winnower. Popular in the pharmaceutical and cosmetics industries because it is a natural oil that does not oxidise easily.

Cocoa mass, cocoa liquor The paste produced by grinding the nibs. Though called liquor it is not alcoholic.

Cocoa solids The collective term for the combination of cocoa mass and cocoa butter. Conventionally the proportion of cocoa butter is not revealed on an ingredients list. For a 100g bar with 70% cocoa solids declared on the label the breakdown could be 62g of ground cocoa nibs and 8g of cocoa butter; or it could be 56g of cocoa and 14g of cocoa butter, in which case it would have a less dense, dark profile, and a richer, more buttery character.

Conch, conching The process of kneading and stirring chocolate to refine and develop its flavour and texture and to remove unwanted acidity. Time taken is the chocolatier's choice – 40 to 70 hours is the typical range. Invented in 1880 by Rodolphe Lindt. See also page 47.

Cooking chocolate Contains little or no cocoa butter. Instead other cheaper fats and lecithin (to stabilise) are used. Bears little relation to chocolate in taste. Widely used for cake decorations as it is cheaper than the real thing, and does not require tempering.

Couverture Term for chocolate supplied to chocolatiers and fondeurs to melt, temper and mould into bars and bonbons. Some fondeurs also blend several couvertures. Supplied in block format, or as buttons for quicker melting, or in liquid form, pre-melted and tempered.

Criollo The finest of the three main types of cacao, with particularly delicate aromas and flavours. It is difficult to grow as it is susceptible to disease. Many of today's Criollos are not pure strains, as they have crossed naturally with other types. See also page 32.

Cru, Grand Cru Term taken from French wine terminology, meaning 'growth' or 'great growth'. Intended to indicate a high-quality chocolate from a named origin. It has no legal status.

Dark chocolate A blend of cocoa mass, sugar and cocoa butter. Starts at 43% cocoa solids in the European Union and 35% in the United States.

Dutch process, dutching The process of treating cocoa nibs, or cocoa mass, with an alkalising agent, invented by the Dutchman Coenraad Van Houten in the early 19th century originally as a means of helping cocoa powder to disperse in hot liquid. It makes the cocoa darker and mellows the flavour. See Cocoa butter.

Fairtrade An organisation, started in the Netherlands in 1988, that guarantees through a labelling scheme better terms and conditions for workers and more sustainable working. Also used as an adjective 'fair trade' to describe an ethical approach to business. See also page 41.

Fermentation The first stage in building the flavour profile of chocolate. The freshly picked beans are scooped out of the pods and yeasts convert the sugars in the juicy mucilage which surrounds the bean into ethanol and acetic acid. With the rise in temperature through fermentation, the bean dies and enzymes can break through the cell walls to start reactions which develop flavour and colour. See also page 36.

Fine or flavour This vague-sounding phrase is a category defined by the ICCO, International Cocoa Organization (*www.icco.org*). Typically only Criollo and Trinitario beans are rated as 'fine or flavour', although Ecuador's Nacional (of Forastero origin) is also included. Total world production of this category of bean is about 5 per cent; the rest is classified as 'bulk'. Currently 17 countries are defined as 'fine or flavour' producers and the list changes from time to time.

Flavanols Naturally occurring antioxidants, members of the flavonoid family, found in cacao.

Fondeur French word meaning 'melter'. Describes a chocolatier who melts couverture and moulds it into bars. Can be a highly skilled activity, blending couvertures and tempering accurately.

Forastero The most widely grown type of cacao bean. Popular for its high yields and disease resistance. Widely grown in Africa. A superior version, Nacional, is grown in Ecuador. See also page 32.

Ganache A blend of chocolate with cream, and usually butter. May be flavoured. Typically coated in chocolate.

Gianduja Finely ground nuts and sugar mixed to a paste with chocolate.

Lecithin An emulsifier, made from soya beans, used to ease the processing of chocolate. Some producers dislike the waxy quality that it can give to the palate of the chocolate, and the fact that it modifies, even slightly, the character of the bean itself. As the soya beans may have been genetically modified, lecithin is not used by producers who want to avoid GMO. See also page 46.

Maltitol A sugar substitute that is considered to be more suitable for people with diabetes than sucrose (sugar). Not a successful ingredient in chocolate, where it gives a cold, metallic effect.

Melangeur Grinder, for grinding cocoa nibs. See also page 47.

Metate Traditional shallow stone dish for pounding cocoa beans, still used in Central America.

Milk chocolate A blend of cocoa mass, sugar and milk powder, usually between 25 and 45% cocoa solids.

Nib The central part of the cocoa bean, after the husk has been removed. Ground to produce cocoa butter and cocoa liquor/mass. A bar 'with nibs' will have crunchy pieces of nibs mixed in.

Organic Like any organic product, organic chocolate has to meet certain standards in order to be certified in its country of origin. Growers of the cacao bean (and sugar, milk powder and vanilla, if relevant) must avoid the use of artificial pesticides and fertilisers.

Raw Chocolate that has not been subjected to the same degree of heating and processing as conventional chocolate, and as a result is higher in antioxidants.

Roasting Critical process in developing aroma and flavour in chocolate. A burnt character can easily spoil the entire batch. See also page 46.

Semisweet chocolate Less dark than bittersweet.

Single estate Indicates that the cacao is high quality and grown in a defined area, with a defined terroir.

Snap The sound of the clean break of a well-tempered chocolate, showing the ordered crystalline structure of the cocoa butter.

Storing In the right environment a dark chocolate bar is a stable product. While the aromas are freshest when young, a plain dark bar will keep for up to 18 months without any sign of deterioration, and it will still be enjoyable for a long time after that. Keep bars apart from strongly flavoured foods, in a cool, dark place, ideally at 12°–16°C (53°–60°F). It is not necessary to freeze chocolate bars, but this can be done by wrapping them in greaseproof paper and then in an airtight container. It is essential to avoid moisture. To defrost, bring slowly back to room temperature before opening the package.

Tempering An essential stage in making fine chocolate. The process of carefully heating and cooling melted chocolate to ensure even, stable distribution of the crystals in the cocoa butter. A poorly tempered bar is dull, can show smears and streaks and is often grainy. See also page 48.

Terroir French word taken from wine terminology. Describes the combination of soil, climate, aspect to the sun, and the influence of the grower that together affect the character of the chocolate, and give it a distinct flavour. See also page 28.

Trinitario One of the three main types of cacao bean. A cross between Criollo and Forastero. See also page 33.

Truffle A blend of chocolate and cream, usually shaped in a small ball or log, and rolled in cocoa powder. May be flavoured with alcohol.

Vanillin A synthetic version of vanilla.

White chocolate Made from cocoa butter, powdered milk and sugar. See also page 41.

Useful Addresses

Many of the producers featured in the Chocolate Directory (see pages 62–227) sell a fine selection of bars, not just their own, and I urge you to visit them. Some of these producers have their own shops and some sell their bars online. On these pages is a personal selection of other shops and online retailers. This list is not intended to be exhaustive: they are either my own choice or recommended by people whose opinions I respect. For chocolate lovers, visiting a new city means seeking out a new chocolate shop. Yet there is nothing worse than trekking across town, only to end up with mediocre chocolate. That is why I hope this list will interest and excite you. Please note that these retailers have been selected because they sell bars, not because of their filled chocolates or patisserie, so some well-known chocolatiers are not listed here. If you have any favourites not listed here, please send me your own recommendations (*www.sarahjaneevans.co.uk*).

AUSTRALIA
Xocolatl (Melbourne)
www.xocolatl.com.au

AUSTRIA
Schokov (Vienna) (online)
www.schokov.com
Xocolat (Vienna, Linz and Baden) *www.xocolat.at*

CANADA
A Taste for Chocolate (online)
www.atasteforchocolate.com

CHILE
Bozzo (Santiago)
www.bozzochocolates.cl
La Fête (Santiago)
www.lafetechocolat.com

GERMANY
Atelier Cacao (Berlin)
www.atelier-cacao.de
Chocolats de luxe (online)
www.chocolats-de-luxe.de
Fassbender & Rausch (Berlin)
www.rausch-schokolade.com
Stolberg Schokoladen (Munich)
www.stolberg-muenchen.de
Xocoatl (Wiesbaden)
www.xocoatl.de

JAPAN
Le Chocolat de H (Tokyo)
www.lcdh.jp

POLAND
Czekoladki Swiata (Warsaw)
www.czekoladkiswiata.pl

SLOVAKIA
Chocotheka (online)
www.chocotheka.sk

SPAIN
Bubó (Barcelona)
www.bubo.es
Xocoa (Barcelona)
www.xocoa-bcn.com

SWITZERLAND
Truffe (Zurich)
www.truffe-zurich.ch
Xocolatl (Basel)
www.xocolatl-basel.ch

UK
Alderwood Chocolate Deli (Saddleworth)
www.chocolatedeli.net
The Chocolate Café (Manchester)
www.chocolate-cafe.co.uk
The Chocolate Society (London) *www.chocolate.co.uk*
Whole Foods Market (London)
www.wholefoodsmarket.com

USA
Biagio Fine Chocolate (Washington, DC)
www.biagiochocolate.com
Bittersweet Café (San Francisco, CA)
www.bittersweetcafe.com
Stocks a wide range of bars, as well as their own
Cacao (Portland, OR)
www.cacaodrinkchocolate.com
Excellent selection of bars and chocolates.
The Candy Store (San Francisco, CA)
www.thecandystoresf.com
Chocolopolis (Seattle, WA)
www.chocolopolis.com
Fog City News (San Francisco, CA)
www.fogcitynews.com
When in SF start at this newsagent for a great selection of bars.
Pair Chocolates (Barrington, IL)
www.pairchocolates.com
Whole Foods Market
www.wholefoodsmarket.com
In a city where there is no destination chocolate bar shop, it is always worth dropping into Whole Foods Market. Stores throughout the US.

Department stores with deli sections are also worth a visit.

CHOCOLATE FESTIVALS

Some of these festivals have closed professional areas.

AUSTRALIA (Melbourne)
Chocolate Rush
www.chocolaterush.com.au

BEIJING, MOSCOW, PARIS, NEW YORK, SHANGHAI, TOKYO
Salon du Chocolat
www.salonduchocolat.fr

ITALY
Eurochocolate Festival
www.eurochocolate.com
Fiera del Cioccolato Artigionale (Florence)
www.fieradelcioccolato.it

UK
Chocolate Week
www.chocolate-week.co.uk
Chocolate Unwrapped
www.chocolateunwrapped.co.uk

USA
Fancy Food Show (New York and San Francisco)
www.specialityfood.com/fancy-food-show
Los Angeles Luxury Chocolate Salon
www.lachocolatesalon.com
Also in Napa, San Francisco and Seattle.

CHOCOLATE MUSEUMS

A small selection of the more interesting museums, and a few commercial ones. Many museums attached to producers' factories can be extremely commercial.

BELGIUM
Museum of Cocoa and Chocolate (Brussels)
www.mucc.be
Choco-story (Bruges)
www.choco-story.be

FRANCE
Chocolatrium Michel Cluizel (Normandy)
www.cluizel.com

GERMANY
Rausch Schokoland (Peine, Hanover)
www.rausch-schokolade.com
Schokoladenmuseum (Cologne)
www.chocolatemuseum-cologne.com

SPAIN
Museu de la Xocolata (Barcelona)
www.pastisseria.cat

UK
Cadbury World (Birmingham)
www.cadburyworld.co.uk

BLOGS AND WEBSITES

There is a very vibrant community of chocolate bloggers. Two websites have been working seriously and longer than most and give a very good overview of the chocolate world –
www.seventypercent.com (British) and
www.chocolatelife.com (US).
www.davidlebovitz.com is a lively food blog, based in Paris. Three enthusiastic chocolate fans are doing a good job in reviewing bars:
chocolateincontext.blogspot.com from a one-time bookshop owner who is keen on chocolate;
chocolateratings.wordpress.com which does what it says: serious about reviewing serious chocolate; and
www.chocablog.co.uk which has regular reports from a UK chocolate fan.
Academy of Chocolate
www.academyofchocolate.org.uk
UK-based. Aims to spread the word about fine chocolate.
The following listings have plenty of interesting reports and reference material.
The International Cocoa Organization *www.icco.org*
World Cocoa Foundation
www.worldcocoafoundation.org
The WCF has a lively blog.

Bibliography

Allen, Brigid (ed.) (1994), *Food: An Oxford Anthology*, Oxford: Oxford University Press

Beckett, Stephen T. (2nd edn 2008), *The Science of Chocolate*, London: Royal Society of Chemistry

Brenner, Joël Glenn (2000), *The Chocolate Wars: Inside the Secret Worlds of Mars & Hershey*, London: Harper Collins

Coady, Chantal (2003), *Real Chocolate*, London: Quadrille; (2006), *The Connoisseur's Guide to Chocolate*, London: Apple Press

Coe, Sophie D and Michael D (1996), *The True History of Chocolate*, London: Thames & Hudson

Dalby, Andrew (2000), *Dangerous Tastes: The Story of Spices*, London: British Museum Press

Doutre-Roussel, Chloé (2005), *The Chocolate Connoisseur*, London: Piatkus

Gordon, Clay (2007), *Discover Chocolate*, New York: Gotham Books

Jayne-Stanes, Sara (1999, rev. edn 2005), *Chocolate: The Definitive Guide*, London: Grub Street

Khodorowsky, Katherine, de Loisy, Olivier and Senderens, Alain (2003), *Chocolat et Grands Crus de Cacao*, Paris: Éditions Solar

Lagorce, Stéphan (2003, Spanish edn), *Los Aromas del Chocolate*, Barcelona: Larousse

Mason, Laura (2004), *Sugar-Plums and Sherbet: The Prehistory of Sweets*, Devon: Prospect Books.

McEwan, Colin and López Luján, Leonardo (eds) (2009), *Moctezuma: Aztec Ruler*, London: British Museum Press

Off, Carol (2006), *Bitter Chocolate: The Dark Side of the World's Most Seductive Sweet*, New York: The New Press

Perry, Sara and Zwinger, Jane (2008), *Deep Dark Chocolate: Decadent Recipes for the Serious Chocolate Lover*, San Francisco: Chronicle Books

Rosenblum, Mort (2006), *Chocolate: A Bittersweet Saga of Dark and Light*, New York: North Point Press

Toussaint-Samat, Maguelonne (2nd edn 2008), *A History of Food*, Oxford: Wiley-Blackwell

Vaughan, J.G. and Geissler, C.A. (1999), *The New Oxford Book of Food Plants*, Oxford: Oxford University Press

Visser, Margaret (1996), *The Rituals of Dinner: The Origins, Evolution, Eccentricities and the Meaning of Table Manners*, London: Penguin Books

Young, Allen M. (rev edn 2007), *The Chocolate Tree: A Natural History of Cacao*, Gainesville: University Press of Florida

Index

Acknowledgments

Author acknowledgments

There are many chocolate lovers and friends who have given me contacts, ideas, and encouragement; who have helped with translation; and shopped for bars. Thank you all: Max Allen; Rosamund Barton and Rupert Ponsonby; Martin Christy of *www.seventypercent.com*; James Cronin; Peter Csizmadia-Honigh; André Dang; Chloé Doutre-Roussel; Stefano Girelli and Victoria Morrall; Simon Harris of Barry-Callebaut; the ICCO; Kate Johns of *www.chocolate-week.co.uk* and the Chocolate Unwrapped festival; Tony Lass of Fox Consultancy Services; Las Madres Irlandesas, who occupy the palace in which Hernán Cortés died in Castilleja de la Cuesta outside Sevilla, Spain, and who started me off in Hernán Cortés' footsteps when they gave me lunch there when I was a student; Marcelo Marasco of Bodegas Septima, Argentina; Sean McLaughlin; Floyd Millar of Cocoa Rhapsody, Australia; Marie-Pierre Moine; Laura Morris; Tony Mycock of HB Ingredients; Daniel Pi, Chief Winemaker of Trapiche wines, Argentina; Christopher Reeves; Nicola Scott-Penard; Lisa Shara Hall; Ivica Sowemimo of *www.chocotheka.sk*; Cocoa Stanes; Richard Stanes; Gary Werner; Scott Wilson of Mediteria; Tsiry Wilkinson; Lyndon Wittingslow.

Every chocolate company featured in these pages has been most generous with their help and assistance. In addition there are chocolate professionals who have given me advice in their personal capacity, and many of them have gone beyond the call of duty in answering my questions and sharing their thoughts. So I would particularly like to thank: Roberto Aguero; Bertil Åkesson; Damian Allsop; Claire Burnett; Chantal Coady; William and Suzue Curley; Mott Green; Keith Hurdman; Philipp Kauffmann; Sara Jayne-Stanes; Bill McCarrick; Art Pollard; Alessio Tessieri; Angus Thirlwell; Paul A Young.

At Anova Books I am really grateful to the design team of Georgie Hewitt and John Heritage; to Maggie Ramsay, for her impressively scrupulous attention to the text, even under the most extreme pressure; and to Fiona Holman, for her clever ideas, her persistence and her warmth. Renowned as the best in the business when it comes to wine books, she has definitely proved herself with chocolate. Together she and Maggie prove that proper old-fashioned editing still survives. Finally I must thank my private in-house chocolate experts, Richard, Consola and Seraphina, for their encouragement and tolerance.

The author and publishers would like to thank all the chocolate producers featured in the book for their generous help with sourcing chocolate bars for the tastings and photography; also Barking Dog Art for the maps and chart and Michael Wicks for photography of the bars.

Picture acknowledgments

Alamy page 21 Advertisement for Suchard chocolate in the magazine *Je sais tout* 1911 France Private Collection **Alter Eco** page 67 **Amedei** page 56 **Amma/Diego Badaró** page 73 **Akesson's** pages 34, 53 **The Bridgeman Art Library** page 2 *Cocoa Tree*, 1993 (acrylic on paper) by Wright, Liz (b.1950), Private Collection; page 10 *Figure from a vessel top in the form of a cocoa (chocolate) deity*, 600-900 AD (slipped and painted earthenware) by Mayan, Indianapolis Museum of Art, USA/Gift of Bonnie and David Ross; page 13 Fol.156v *Montezuma II (1466-1520) and his envoys to the Spanish conquerors*, 1579 (vellum) by Duran, Diego (16th century), Biblioteca Nacional, Madrid, Spain/Giraudon; page 14 *Mexican Indian Preparing Chocolate*, from the Codex Tuleda, 1553 (vellum) by Mexican School, (16th century), Museo de America, Madrid, Spain; page 15 *How the Natives of New Spain Prepared Cacao for Chocolate* (engraving) by French School, (16th century) Bibliothèque Nationale, Paris, France/Giraudon; page 16 *Still Life with a Bowl of Chocolate*, or *Breakfast with Chocolate*, c.1640 (oil on canvas) by Zurbarán, Juan de (1620-49) (attr. to), Musée des Beaux-Arts et d'Archéologie, Besançon, France/Giraudon; page 17 Fabric depicting a chocolate pot and a teapot, Lyon Workshop, c.1730 (silk) by French School, (18th century), Musée de la Ville de Paris, Musée Carnavalet, Paris, France/Giraudon; page 19 *Taking tea at the White House*, 1787 (hand-coloured aquatint) by Rowlandson, Thomas (1756-1827) © Museum of London, UK; page 20 W. Baker & Co., Dorchester, Mass. (colour litho) by Stark, D. (fl.1865) © Boston Athenaeum, USA; page 23 Collectors' card from 'Chocolat Guerin-Boutron', c.1900 (colour litho) by French School, (20th century), Musée Nationale des Arts et Traditions Populaires, Paris, France/Archives Charmet; page 24 An American soldier giving chocolate to a small boy in occupied Germany, 1945, © SZ Photo/SV-Bilderdienst; page 171 *Portrait of Montezuma II* (oil on canvas) by European School, (16th century), Palazzo Pitti, Florence, Italy; page 205 *Sir Hans Sloane* (1660-1753) engraved by William Home Lizars (1788-1859) for Sloane's memoir in Jardine's *Naturalist's Library*, c.1833-45 (engraving) by Kneller, Sir Godfrey (1646-1723) (after); **Cacao Sampaka** page 93; **Chocolate Santander** page 99; **Chocolate Unwrapped 2009/Chocolate Week** *www.chocolate-week.co.uk* (photo James Boyer Smith) page 61; **Claudio Corallo** pages 30, 33; **François Pralus** pages 8–9, 37, 54; **The Grenada Chocolate Company** pages 47 (both), 49 (all); **Haigh's Chocolates** page 137; **Hotel Chocolat** page 139; **Kallari** pages 1, 35 (both); **Mast Brothers** page 163; **Kim Naylor** page 113; **Original Beans** pages 31, 32, 36, 42, 45, 52, 55; **Paul A Young** page 183.